Content

C000148067

Foreword

From time to time aspects of adoption present us with difficult terrain for which there appear to be no clear maps and few guidelines to follow. When this happens you are likely to find that Catherine Macaskill undertakes a study which maps out a clear way forward.

In 1985, with her book *Against the Odds: Adopting Children with Disabilities*, Catherine broke new ground and inspired professionals to consider family placement as an option for children who had previously been considered 'unadoptable'. *Adopting or Fostering a Sexually Abused Child*, published six years later in 1991, was a godsend to those of us trying to find ways of giving effective support to families looking after some very traumatised children. It remains a valuable source today.

Needless to say, when Catherine wrote to *Parents for Children* to enquire whether we might consider sponsoring her research into an aspect of current practice, we wanted to support her work. Her pilot study interviews with families who had adopted or fostered through *Parents for Children* and with the children themselves were revealing. It became apparent that the tangled web of contact between the children and their families of origin, including brothers and sisters and half siblings, grandparents and aunts and uncles, previous carers as well as birth parents was posing problems with which the comparatively few studies about contact had grappled.

This point had been made, tellingly, by Quinton and colleagues, 1997.

In our present state of knowledge it is seriously misleading to think that what we know about contact is at a level of sophistication to allow us to make confident assertions about the benefits to be gained from it, regardless of family circumstances and relationships. At least in the case of permanent placements the social experiment that is currently underway needs to be recognised as an experiment, not as an example of the development of evidence-based practice. It is important that the effects of this experiment are properly evaluated.

This publication is about the day-to-day dilemmas associated with face-to-face contact for adopters, foster carers, children and professionals. It examines the issue of preparation of children and permanent foster and adoptive families for contact; the perspective of children who can talk from personal experience about real experiences of contact with their birth relatives; the importance of confidentiality as a means of safeguarding children from further abuse; particular dilemmas in sibling contact; and the very difficult theme of how to provide an effective support service extending beyond adoption. These and a host of other insights into what helps contact to succeed, and some of the pitfalls, make this book essential reading.

I am sure you will find the content lucid and compelling. For both families and for practitioners in the field, it will be an invaluable guide through the complexities of contact for many years to come.

Karen Irving
Chief Executive
Parents for Children

Special Acknowledgement of *Parents for Children*

This research study took three years to complete. Such a project would not have been possible without considerable financial input. I am especially grateful to the Executive Committee of *Parents for Children* for agreeing to fund the initial sixteen months of this project. This enabled the study to be established; a pilot project about face-to-face contact based on *Parents for Children*'s own work to be completed; and for the research study to be extended to include other statutory and voluntary agencies. The final twenty months of the project including telephone interviews, data analysis and the preparation of the manuscript for publication were self-financed.

I am particularly indebted to Karen Irving, Chief Executive at *Parents for Children* for being the inspiration behind this research study. She perceived the need for this work to be undertaken at a time when professionals continue to search for answers to many complex questions surrounding the issue of contact between children in permanent placement and their birth relatives.

Parents for Children

Parents for Children

Parents for Children was set up in 1976. This innovative agency has always been at the cutting edge of new developments in family placement work. It has proved to be an inspiration to other voluntary and statutory agencies as it has demonstrated that many children who had previously been considered 'unadoptable' could be successfully placed with adoptive families. Initially its success was mainly through achieving family placement for children with severe learning difficulties.

Today, after 25 years of credible professional practice the work of the agency continues to thrive. A very high proportion of the children who are currently being placed have suffered emotional trauma and the challenges facing professionals and prospective families are enormous. New projects have been established to meet the diverse needs of children, including a specialist fostering scheme, a respite care project and a specialist project for the placement of sibling groups. As the work progresses into the 21st century it continues to be a demonstration model of good practice in family placement work for others to emulate.

CHAPTER 1

Introduction

Contact is a buzzword. It is a concept that now permeates adoption and fostering practice and is likely to do so throughout the 21st century. Today any adoptive family who feel sceptical about the principle of an adopted child retaining contact with birth family members is likely to be viewed with professional uncertainty and even disapproval. Some professionals are strong advocates of the benefits for adopted children associated with contact. Others have dared to voice caution. Everyone involved in this debate is unanimous about the necessity of extending professional knowledge on this crucial subject. This book, based on a research study delves into the experiences of adoptive and foster families as they talk from personal experience about how contact has impacted on their lives. It is based on the premise that the views of those closest to a critical event are significant and uniquely credible.

The fact that contact with the birth family can be an integral part of an adoption plan is a reminder of the speed and magnitude of the changes that have occurred in adoption in Britain during the past three decades. Prior to the 1970s, only healthy babies were considered eligible for adoption. There was an emphasis on secrecy and confidentiality and adoption inevitably required a 'clean break' from the birth family. The theories of Goldstein, Freud and Solnit (1973) were influential. They mirrored the views of Bowlby (1951) and emphasised the importance to children of having an exclusive relationship with their adoptive parents. The concept of children having to relate simultaneously to more than one set of parent figures was perceived as potentially damaging to any child.

The adoption of healthy infants is now almost obsolete. This has been influenced by the increased availability of abortion and more liberal attitudes towards the status of single parenthood. During the early 1970s the 'permanence' movement was developed for 'hard to place' children. These were school age children with troubled histories, sibling groups, teenagers, children from minority ethnic backgrounds and children with learning difficulties. Initially permanence was synonymous with adoption but gradually there was a growing awareness of the need for a diversity of permanent fostering schemes to meet the complex needs of very difficult children. Adoption for this group of children usually meant a termination of all birth family links. In fact grieving and letting go of the birth family were perceived as essential prerequisites to the process of bonding with an adoptive family.

Contact emerged as a professional issue in the late 1970s when adoption became an option for many school age children in the care system, with significant birth family links. Children and birth parents became vocal about their wish to retain these vital connections. Black children began to be placed trans-racially in white families. This aroused concern about the potential loss of their racial identity. Professionals began to ask, 'Could some retention of birth family connection be one way of minimising this loss?' Within the context of foster care there was also renewed interest in the subject of 'access'. Rowe and Lambert's study *Children Who Wait* (1973) was highly influential and ignited a new professional awareness of the significance of 'access'. They presented a daunting picture of the length of time children drifted in the care system and were unequivocal about the importance of 'access' as a facilitating factor for children who achieved successful rehabilitation within their birth family.

The vital importance of adopted children knowing about their origins owes much to the work of Triseliotis (1973). The implementation in 1976 of The Children Act (1975) permitting adoptees to gain access to their original birth certificate was a significant milestone. Throughout the 1980s there was a growing awareness of the importance of more openness and less secrecy for all participants in adoption.

The Children Act (1989) implemented in 1991 in England and Wales changed the direction of childcare work and especially influenced fostering practice. The Act introduced the concept of 'contact' to replace 'access'. It gave a new emphasis to the rights and responsibilities of birth parents. It required statutory agencies to work in partnership with parents. Rehabilitation with the birth family was to be the principal objective for any child cared for by the local authority. When rehabilitation failed a key feature of childcare practice was to be the establishment of a plan for contact between children and their birth family. In all contact decisions the welfare of the child was to be paramount.

This study aims to place the subject of contact within the current childcare scene in Britain. This is particularly important because so much of the literature supporting contact is concerned with infant adoption in the USA and New Zealand. In New Zealand the idea simply involved some participation by the birth family in the choice of placement with an information exchange about the progress of the child. There is a danger of wrenching research findings about contact and infant adoption from their context and inappropriately applying them to adoption of 'hard to place' children. Two important features of current adoption practice, which need to be taken into account, are:
1. Over 40 per cent of adopted children are aged five years or older at the time of placement (Dance, Cullen and Collier, 1997).
2. A high proportion of this group of 'hard to place' children have been adopted because of serious parenting difficulties by their birth parents

who have frequently been perpetrators of neglect, rejection, physical and sexual abuse (Quinton, Rushton, Dance and Mayes, 1998). Children are therefore likely to have very problematic attachment relationships with their birth family. These difficulties are likely to impinge on any contact relationship.

The research study focuses on how contact impacts on permanent placements of children. The majority of placements included in the study are adoption: a smaller number are permanent fostering.

Clear definitions of the meaning of contact are also very important. The SSI Study into Post Adoption Contact in the North of England (1995) highlights the problems associated with a lack of agreed language to describe different forms of post adoption contact. The term contact can include a range of options such as:

- An exchange of Christmas and birthday cards sent directly or through social services.
- An annual letter from adoptees to birth parents.
- An exchange of photographs.
- Infrequent or frequent meetings either formally supervised by social services or informally arranged.

Different contact arrangements may exist between the adoptee and a whole range of different relatives. Arrangements can be immensely complex. Triseliotis (1985) draws attention to the fact that terms such as semi-open adoption; open adoption; and adoption with contact are often used interchangeably and sometimes misleadingly. Other researchers describe openness as being on a continuum with the arrangements changing over time in response to changing needs and circumstances. McRoy (1991)found in her nationwide study of 132 adopted children in the USA that there were five major categories and 33 sub categories to describe the variety of open arrangements. In contrast this study is single minded. It focuses exclusively on one form of direct contact where face-to-face meetings occur with a birth relative.

This is a subject that evokes a lively debate. Those who argue against it fear that:

- Multiple attachments will create confusion for children.
- The threat of harm to the child or to the new parents may undermine the placement.
- Birth parents need to be helped towards closure as the best way of dealing with feelings of loss and guilt.
- Demands placed on the new parents will adversely affect the recruitment of new adopters.
- It is too risky to make such complex placements without adequate professional skills and resources which need to extend far beyond adoption.

Gerrilyn Smith, a clinical psychologist with extensive experience of working with children who have been sexually abused, argues that children who have suffered the impact of trauma and abuse have the right to leave their past behind during their formative years in order to allow them to form healthy new attachments. Writing in 1995 on the subject 'Do Children Have a Right to Leave their Past Behind them?' she states that 'Continued contact with abusive families, rather than letting children move forward, can pull them back to their past'.

Some professionals like Ryburn (1992, 1994 and 1998) have become strong advocates of the benefits of contact. Others quote relevant research, sometimes selectively, to underline their unqualified enthusiasm. In the largest survey of adoption and permanent foster care ever undertaken in Britain involving 1165 placements Fratter, Rowe, Sapsford and Thoburn (1991) found that birth family contact was the single factor that could be identified as enhancing the stability of placements. Fratter (1996) concluded her research study into contact with an enthusiastic endorsement of its benefits for all parties involved. Those who are eager to promote contact argue that:

- Children need to be connected to their biological and historical past if they are going to grow up with a positive self image and identity.
- Contact satisfies the child's need for information and prevents the unhealthy idealisation of the birth family.
- Contact counters the child's feelings of rejection and self blame through evidence of the birth family's continued interest.
- Contact is said to enhance the adoptive parent's sense of entitlement to the child, legitimising their parenting role and making it easier to talk to the child about the nature of their relationship.

This study does not confine itself to an examination of birth parent contact. It looks more broadly at contact with a range of birth relatives including birth parents, grandparents, uncles, aunts, cousins and siblings. It also examines placements where children have multiple contacts with different family members.

There is a scarcity of literature that examines the complex dynamics inherent in contact between siblings. Those who have written on the subject tend to emphasise the gaps that exist in professional knowledge. Kossonen (1996) has played a significant role in evidencing how frequently sibling contact is lost to a child in the care system. Wedge and Mantle (1991) point out that, 'The relevance of sibling relationships to human development is a largely unknown subject'.

In Beckett's 1993 study into local authority planning and decision making for looked after siblings she found that there was a worrying lack of statutory policies and guidelines governing sibling placements and a lack of strategy for promoting contact between separated siblings. Despite the lack of policy and practice models which reflect best practice, social workers who participated in this study were eager to portray a picture of sibling contact as being relatively straightforward and producing positive results for everyone concerned. As this study focuses on the minutiae of sibling contact, some complex issues are raised which rarely have an easy resolution.

The fact that our knowledge in the area of contact between older children in permanent placement and their birth relatives is still at an embryonic stage is highlighted in a useful summary of research knowledge on this topic by Quinton et al. (1997).

> *In our present state of knowledge it is seriously misleading to think that what we know about contact is at a level of sophistication to allow us to make confident assertions about the benefits to be gained from it regardless of family circumstances and relationships. At least in the case of permanent placements the social experiment that is currently underway needs to be recognised as an experiment, not as an example of evidence based practice.*

Despite the fact that our knowledge about the impact of contact on children is imprecise it is clear that the incidence of cases where contact is occurring is increasing. In the 1995 SSI study of Post-Adoption Contact *Moving The Goalposts* which surveyed the adoption work of 37 social services Departments and 14 voluntary adoption agencies in the north of England they found that in 70 per cent of cases either direct or indirect contact was being maintained between adopted children and their birth relatives after an Adoption Order had been granted.

One specialist social worker who was interviewed for this study and highly committed to the concept of contact expressed concern about how ideologies are translated into day-to-day practice:

> *As far as contact is concerned I sometimes feel as if things are spiralling out of control. The adoption team in which I work get ridiculous requests for contact. Things are not thought through. A lot of social workers have so little dealings with adoption. They feel that they're following through The Children Act. The worrying thing is that they haven't thought through the importance of confidentiality for the adoptive family. The degree of contact requested and the timing of contact do not take account of the need for a child to make an attachment, or for adopters to claim the child. They haven't thought about the pressure on the placement due to the reality of contact. There's a need for a balanced approach but sadly that balance is often missing.*

CHAPTER 2

Setting up the Study

General aim

The aim of the study was to undertake a detailed analysis of the factors that:
- Enable face-to-face contact between children in permanent placement and their birth relatives to work satisfactorily.
- Prevent face-to-face contact between children in permanent placement and their birth relatives from working satisfactorily.

Specific aim

The specific aim of the study was to examine the day-to-day impact on adopters and foster carers and on adoptees and foster children of:
- The implementation by professionals of contact plans.
- Planning and preparation for contact.
- Any difficulties that occurred and how they were managed.
- The level and quality of support available and whether significant gaps existed in service provision.

The study

The study was initiated through a pilot project on face-to-face contact undertaken by the author during 1999. It focussed exclusively on the work of *Parents for Children*, a voluntary adoption agency in London set up in 1976 to pioneer adoption for some of the 'hardest to place' children in Britain. The work of the pilot project was extended to form the main study through the participation of additional voluntary and statutory agencies. A total of six voluntary adoption agencies and three social services departments agreed to take part (see Appendix 1 for details of participating agencies).

It quickly became apparent that the number of black and mixed parentage children and families in the study was quite small. In order to ensure that ethnic issues were included in the study an approach was made to Adoption UK to identify some additional same-race placements.

Selecting a sample for study

The focus of the main study was:
- Permanent placements including long term fostering and adoption.
- Children who were at least four years at the time of placement. One exception was sibling placements where at least one child was required to have attained four years at the time of placement; the other siblings could be younger.

- Children who had suffered emotional trauma. Children with severe learning difficulties were excluded.
- Children were required to have had at least one face-to-face contact with a birth relative since placement in order to be included in the study.
- The term 'birth relative' was not confined to birth parent. It included any member of the extended family.
- All the placements occurred during the 1990s.

Each voluntary agency and social services department was asked to undertake the task of selecting families to participate in the study. The guidelines used are entitled *Criteria for Selection of Families and Steps to Follow* (see details in Appendix 2).

Identifying families proved to be quite an onerous and painstaking task as there was rarely a computerised system whereby families who had face-to-face contact could be easily identified. Another complicating factor was that a number of long standing adoptive families were engaged in contact arrangements independent of the placing agency and staff were unsure about whether they met the criteria for the study. Most participating agencies decided to nominate a key member of staff to undertake essential groundwork.

Although the original plan was to ask each agency to nominate exactly the same number of families this proved to be rather impractical. Negotiating with each agency on an individual basis about the numbers that they could realistically nominate worked better. When the process of selection was complete a letter was sent from the agency encouraging adopters and foster carers to reply directly to the researcher.

In order to ensure that as many families as possible participated in the study those who did not respond to the researcher in the first instance were contacted again through the placing agency. This turned out to be a useful way of augmenting the number of families participating in the study.

Response from families
Figure 1 illustrates the number of families who were asked to participate in the study. The response rate from the voluntary agencies was 57 out of a

	Number of families asked to participate	Number of families who agreed to be interviewed	Number of families followed up by social work interviews	Total
Voluntary agencies	73 families (97 children)	42 families (63 children)	15 families (18 children)	57 families (81 children)
Social services	43 families (50 children)	10 families (14 children)	9 families (11 children)	19 families (25 children)

Figure 1: Response rate from voluntary and statutory agencies

possible 73 families (78 per cent) and included interviews about 81 out of 97 children (83 per cent). The response rate from social services was 19 out of 43 families (44 per cent) and included interviews about 25 out of 50 children (50 per cent). Attempts to enhance the number of black or mixed parentage families through Adoption UK proved disappointing. It became apparent that many of the black families on the database had adopted much younger children. Only six could be identified who met the criteria for the study. Of these, only one agreed to participate despite Adoption UK making more than one attempt to encourage families to contribute to the research project.

Total sample

Families	Children
76	106

Figure 2: Total sample

The total number of families represented in the study was 76. As some families had adopted or fostered more than one child where face-to-face contact had occurred, the study comprised 106 children (see Figure 2).

Gender of child
Although no attempt was made to balance the proportion of boys and girls the total sample comprised an even distribution with 53 boys and 53 girls.

Age of child at time of placement

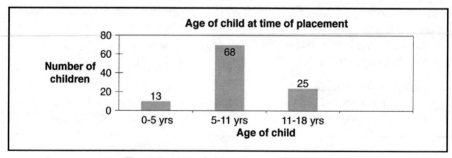

Figure 3a: Age of child at time of placement

All the children were between four years and 16 years old when they joined their new families with the exception of six children who were younger than four years. They were included as they were part of a sibling group.

Age of child at time of research study
By the time the research was undertaken only one child was under five years and five foster or adoptive children were over 18. Four of those over 18 were still living with their foster or adoptive family. One young person was living

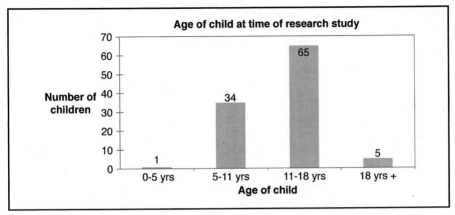

Figure 3b: Age of child at time of research study

independently in close proximity to her adopters who continued to provide regular support.

Types of families

Couples	Single parents
49	27

Figure 4: Type of families

The study comprised 49 couples, 30 of whom had no birth children. Twelve of these 30 couples had adopted or fostered additional children besides the child who was the focus of this study while a further three were in the process of applying for another child at the time of the study. Twenty-three single parents were female and four were male.

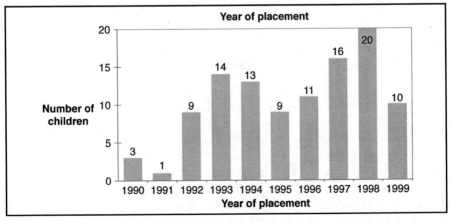

Figure 5: Year of placement

Length of placement

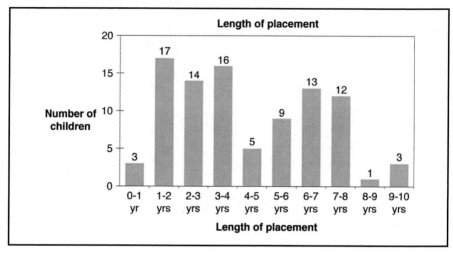

Figure 6: Length of placement

All the placements occurred during the 1990s. 103 placements had occurred since the implementation of The Children Act in 1991 (see Figure 5).

The placements varied in length. The shortest duration was six months and the longest was just over nine years (see Figure 6).

Ethnic background of children and families
The study included 13 children from minority ethnic backgrounds, and among them were Asian, African or African Caribbean children and children of mixed parentage. Eleven children were placed in same-race placements and two were placed trans-racially. Of the 11 children in same-race placements eight were placed on a long term fostering basis rather than adoption.

The legal basis of contact
In adoption cases all contact arrangements were voluntary with the exception of one case where a Section 8 contact order (Children Act 1989) was granted at the same time as an Adoption Order. In this particular case there had been no plan for contact with birth relatives at the time of the adoption placement. However the adopters were convinced due to the girl's level of distress at losing her birth family that some degree of contact was in her best interests. They succeeded in convincing the Guardian ad Litem and later the court that this viewpoint was well founded.

It was interesting to note that a number of adopters were under the impression that contact arrangements had been legally established by the court when this was in fact not the case. This misapprehension had occurred because some discussion about contact issues had occurred in court on the day of the Adoption Hearing.

Fostering placements were different because in all cases the level and degree of contact was established either by the local authority or by the court as part of formal care proceedings.

Background factors

The background histories of the children make sad reading with every form of abuse being perpetrated. A quick glance at the birth parent's own history is sufficient to indicate how often an abusive family history had repeated itself. Many birth parents had had very disturbed childhoods themselves. Inadequate parenting and parental rejection were too often the norm with issues such as physical and sexual abuse being recurring themes. Some had absconded from home at an early age and attempted to live rough; others drifted into a life of prostitution and self degradation; many had been in and out of the care system, leaving them emotionally immature, lacking self esteem and totally unprepared for the demands of parenthood. Against this type of background children had very little chance of any semblance of stability.

The case records of the children in the study are marked by emotive language. Phrases predominate like, 'They were grossly neglected' or 'They had a highly disturbed childhood'. Malnourishment reached the stage of starvation in extreme circumstances. Material conditions were often far from adequate with sometimes the most basic requirements missing such as lighting, heating and bedding. Methods of punishment were extremely damaging. It is hard to fathom in an enlightened 21st century how a child could be kept for days cooped up in a cage or that children would literally be chained to prevent childhood misdemeanours. One birth mother who was so exasperated by her four-year-old child's behaviour punished him by forcing him to swallow a whole chocolate gateau and twelve yoghurts washed down with Fairy Liquid. Sometimes parents reached the end of their tether and completely abandoned their child. For one mother that crisis occurred on her son's fourth birthday. She took her three children to a birthday party but never returned to collect them. Sometimes when family life reached a very low point one of the older siblings assumed a quasi-parental role and was the first person to alert the police or social services. One boy talked about this crisis when he was interviewed for this research study. It was clear that many years later he continued to carry a disproportionate amount of guilt for having 'split' the family unit.

Seventy-two children (68 per cent) were either victims of physical abuse within their birth family or witnessed extreme violence in their home. Physical abuse towards children included:

- attempts to smother, suffocate or drown the child
- burn marks on the child's body
- placing the child's head down the toilet
- tying to a chair
- severe beatings
- torture
- serious threats to kill

Several children witnessed a cruel death in their family and in one instance a young child watched his mother commit suicide by throwing herself from her bedroom window.

Seventy-one children (67 per cent) had been victims of sexual abuse within their birth family. In 30 instances it was not just a case of one family member perpetrating abuse but rather that the child was caught up in the activities of a familial paedophile ring. The members of these paedophile rings were never strangers. They were always family members and in some cases networks of family friends had also been drawn into the sex ring activity. Some sexual practices were bizarre, involving a range of sinister satanic rituals.

Twenty-three children (22 per cent) had grown up in a birth family where at least one birth parent suffered from a psychiatric condition. In 43 instances (40 per cent) the care of children had been adversely affected by parental misuse of alcohol or drugs and there were a number of incidents of parents administering drugs or alcohol to their child. In 16 cases the birth mother had a history of prostitution. In 28 cases a birth parent or older sibling had served or was serving a prison sentence for a range of offences, including theft, fraud, shoplifting, car crimes, assault, murder or manslaughter of a child and a range of sexual offences. Six birth mothers and five birth fathers were convicted Schedule 1 offenders. In other situations members of the extended family were Schedule 1 offenders.

Sixty-two children (58 per cent) had experienced previous disruptions of family placement. Twenty-two children had been in short term fostering placements that had been disrupted. Forty children had been in a permanent placement that had been disrupted: 23 were adopted: 17 were in long term fostering. The most common reasons presented either by social workers or adopters and foster carers for the placement being disrupted were:

- Unsuccessful attempts to place siblings together with sexualised behaviour between siblings being a recurring problem.
- Unmanageable behavioural difficulties.
- A child making an allegation of abuse against their carer or members of the carer's extended family.

Some children had lived through several disruptions in their placement and in a few instances the number extended to six.

Adoption and fostering placements

Adoption finalised	Adoption pending	Adoption delayed	Adoption changed to long term fostering	Long term fostering	Adoption disruption	Fostering disruption
64	9	2	1	17	11	2

Total number of placements = 106.

Figure 7: Adoption versus fostering

All the placements in the study were made with a plan for permanence. Eighty-six of the 106 placements (81 per cent) were in adoption: twenty (19 per cent) were in long term fostering (see Figure 7). In the three cases where adoption was either delayed or changed to long term fostering this was because the adoptive family was struggling to handle behavioural difficulties exhibited by the child. In one of these cases the adoptive mother was adamant that contact with birth parents was the principal factor that was triggering these uncontrollable episodes and destabilising the placement.

It was not always easy to determine why fostering rather than adoption was chosen as the childcare plan. Some children were adamant that they did not want adoption because of a deep-rooted loyalty to their birth family. One 12-year-old would not countenance the idea of changing her surname because for her such a step was associated with disloyalty to her family of origin. Racial issues affected whether the plan was adoption or fostering. One experienced adoption manager talked in detail about how difficult it was for her staff team to recruit black or mixed race adopters for school age children. Advertising for black or mixed race foster carers was in her experience more likely to yield a positive response. Professionals also had a much higher expectation about the level and type of contact that they could ask foster carers rather than adopters to manage. One specialist foster carer had worked hard to retain regular contact with a birth father who had a history of violence, imprisonment and of threatening social services staff. The social worker for this family expressed the view that she would not have expected an adoptive family to manage such a volatile situation. On the other hand she felt justified in asking a specialist foster carer to manage these demands especially as he was receiving an enhanced fostering fee.

Disruptions

Thirteen disruptions to placement feature in the study including 11 adoption and two fostering placements. There were a number of reasons for disruption including:

- sexualised behaviour towards a birth child
- another adopted child being adversely affected
- uncontrollable levels of violence and disruptive behaviour
- the child's inability to meet adopter's expectations

Some families were described as 'out of their depths'. In two instances social services terminated the placement although this was contrary to the adopter's wishes: in one the adopters methods of handling challenging behaviour was perceived as damaging to the child: in the other a crisis was ignited when the adopters were found guilty of an incident of non-accidental injury. In five of the 13 disruptions difficulties ensuing from contact with birth parents was highlighted either by the adopter, foster carer or social worker as a major factor that contributed to the breakdown of the placement.

Contact with whom?

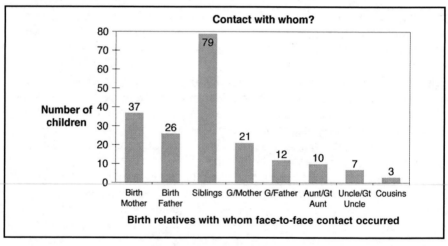

Figure 8: Contact with whom?

Figure 8 portrays the number of children who had contact with each birth relative. As many children had contact with quite a number of different birth relatives the numbers represented in the chart far exceed the 106 children in the study. Most birth parents who retained contact with their children were living separately. Despite separation, some birth parents visited their child together whilst other birth parents met their child at different times and at separate venues.

Some children were in contact with as many as six different birth relatives. Sometimes the arrangements were very formal with close supervision while at other times a very flexible unsupervised system existed. One 12-year-old adoptee retained contact with her birth mother, grandfather, grandmother, aunt, uncle and her great aunt and uncle. Another 14-year-old boy had 11 siblings; the fact that the six siblings with whom he kept in touch were all living in different foster and adoptive families spread over wide geographical distances made the practical arrangements for contact immensely complex.

Method of study

The key participants in the study were people who were able to talk from personal experience about the satisfactory or unsatisfactory nature of contact. The views of the following people were central:

- Adopters or foster carers who had experience of caring for children where face-to-face contact with a birth relative had occurred.
- Children and young people who had experienced face-to-face contact with a birth relative while living with their adoptive or foster family.

It was vital to ensure that data about adopters or foster carers who failed to respond could also be included in the study. It was reasonable to assume that those who did respond might feel more positively about contact than those who failed to reply. In every single case attempts were made to undertake interviews with social workers who knew the non-responding families. Both telephone and face-to-face interviews were deployed in interviews with social workers depending on geographical location. There were certain circumstances where this type of interview was not feasible either because the social worker who worked with the family had left the agency or because the adoptive/foster family was functioning so independently that information about contact arrangements was completely unknown.

It quickly became apparent that these interviews with social workers were a useful adjunct to the study. With a subject as complex as contact it is probably not surprising to discover that attitudes to contact evidenced in family interviews and social work interviews were not completely polarised. A range of positives and negatives emerged in both groups of interviews. However, there were instances in social work interviews where enormous contact problems had occurred. Some social work interviews focussed on disrupted placements where the family had not responded possibly because they may have found the disruption too painful to discuss. Some families had fundamental disagreements with their placing agency and broken relationships had not been healed. Such friction was affecting some contact plans. One family had terminated contact stating that they did not feel that it was in their children's interests and were fighting a legal challenge from the birth family at the time when information about the research had arrived. Naturally, taking part in a research study on contact was a low priority for them at a time when all their energy was being diverted towards a very complex court case. However, the complexities of this case proved to be relevant research data.

Interviews with adopters and foster carers

A semi-structured interview schedule was used with adopters and foster carers in the relaxed atmosphere of their own homes. When a family had adopted or fostered more than one child who met the criteria for inclusion in the study, a separate interview was undertaken on each child. The one exception to this was sibling placements where information about all the siblings was obtained through one interview.

The interview schedule posed questions about adopter's attitudes to and experience of contact, preparation for contact, day-to-day difficulties and how these were managed, whether they felt professional services were adequate, the availability, or otherwise, of systems of support and their views about improving current services or instigating new resources.

At the conclusion of the interview, the question of interviewing children was raised. The issue of contact was of course especially sensitive for the children represented in this study who had often suffered abuse within their birth family. A deliberate decision was therefore made to gain the confidence of the adults first before broaching the subject of undertaking direct research interviews with children. It was hoped that if adopters and foster carers felt comfortable with the sensitive way in which their interview was conducted that they would feel more confident about giving permission for children to voice their opinions. The research tools that were going to be used with the children were shared openly with the adopters and foster carers. This seemed to have an empowering effect.

Some adopters and foster carers were immediately positive and responded in the following ways:

He'd feel really honoured to be asked.

She'd love the one-to-one attention.

I'm sure he'd speak to you because he wants to tell the whole world about his adoption.

Others were much more cautious and replied:

He doesn't like speaking about it.

I'm afraid that it would upset her too much.

They just wouldn't have a clue; they know that these people coming to see them are kind of special but they don't understand about mummies and daddies.

Some people worried about the impact on their child of meeting a total stranger and raised the question, 'Would she think there was a hidden agenda?' In some instances the timing of the request was clearly not right because the child was either caught up in a contact wrangle or going through an especially problematical phase. However, it was clear in other instances where approval was not granted that adopters and foster carers were themselves highly vulnerable and worried that they might have difficulty managing the aftermath. It was obviously vital to respect adopters' and foster carers' views about whether children could be interviewed and impossible to proceed without their wholehearted approval.

Requests to professionals to interview children

Thirteen children had lived through a disruption to placement. It only proved feasible to interview two children and young people in this category. Where social services or residential staff permission was required this was difficult to obtain and was largely brushed aside with the comment, 'It would be much too upsetting for the child'. In the case of one 13-year-old girl whose adoption placement had been disrupted, the adopters were continuing to see her. They discussed the research study with her and enquired whether she might like to contribute her thoughts and ideas. She readily agreed. However the Head of the girl's residential unit declined permission for her to participate, stating that she had discussed the matter with the girl and that she was completely disinterested.

Direct interviews with children and young people

The 37 children and young people who agreed to participate were told that the researcher was writing a book about adoption and that some of their ideas would be included in a book. This was exciting. During the interview some children asked quizzically, 'Will the book only be about me?' A number looked crestfallen when they discovered that other children were also participating.

Before embarking on the interview children were told that they could stop the interview at any time and that they should not feel pressurised to answer any question. They were also told that the material that they shared would be confidential and not passed on to their adopters, foster carers, or members of their birth family.

Children and young people were asked by the researcher, 'Do you have a Life Story Book? Could you tell me about the different photographs in your book and particularly about yourself when you were growing up. Begin with a photograph of you as a baby'.

The children loved to talk about themselves. As they turned the pages and talked about different photographs it was relatively easy to open up a conversation about the birth family. Some Life Story Books also contained certificates that children had been awarded for art competitions, cycling proficiency and different sporting events. This enabled the conversation to be diverted at various points on to less intense matters. The aspects that children talked about from their Life Story Books were their choice and so this gave the child a degree of control over the interview process. When a Life Story Book did not exist, photographs of the birth family were used as an alternative. Some children talked at great length about difficulties while living in their birth family while others were much more reserved about what information they wanted to divulge. This approach proved to be an excellent way of engaging with children about such a sensitive topic. It also gave the researcher an opportunity to assess each child's ability and time to think about the best way to individualise each interview.

The second part of the interview process was participative. It involved using a workbook or story book, specially prepared for this research study, entitled *Ben The Dog* that narrated the story of a dog who had an adoptive family and a birth family. At various points throughout the story children were invited to help the dog find solutions to difficulties with contact issues and at other times Ben asked them about their family situation. The workbook was designed in a flexible way so that children had the choice of drawing, writing their own story or narrating a story for the researcher to record. This adaptability made it versatile enough to use with children of differing abilities. Finally a simple interview questionnaire was used. This was designed mainly for teenagers although some children as young as nine asked if they could attempt to answer the questions and managed to do so very successfully. Questions were posed like:

- *When you knew that you were moving to your new family did anyone ever ask you if you wanted to keep in touch with people in your birth family?*
- *Were plans for contact with your birth relatives ever written down for you? Do you think that it is a good or bad idea to have the plan in writing?*
- *Tell me about a time when something really good happened during contact with your birth family?*
- *Tell me about a time when something difficult happened during contact with your birth family?*
- *Who gets the most out of contact meetings?*
- *If another child asked you, 'What's it like having two families?' what would you say?*
- *Do you think anything new needs to be set up to help young people who are adopted or fostered to keep in contact with their birth relatives?*

Children's attitude to research interviews

The children and young people who participated seemed to appreciate the opportunity to do so. It was clear that most thrived on one-to-one attention. Karl (14) was so disappointed when the interview finished that he pleaded, 'Please make up some extra questions especially for me'. Although the children had been told that they could stop the interview at any time, most children seemed eager to answer every question and one girl who had been grossly abused by a number of birth relatives said, 'I'd really like to answer everything even though it might be quite hard'. Matthew (15), whose birth mother had terminated contact after a sexual incident between him and his younger siblings, stopped when he was on the verge of talking about this and said, 'I'd rather not tell you about that because I don't know you well enough'. Mandy (17) spent additional time during her interview trying to make sense of all her 'love and hate' feelings towards her birth brother who had sexually abused her ten years previously when they were in residential care together.

Each interview had to be handled with immense sensitivity because of the topic that was being addressed. It was challenging for the researcher to find ways of utilising the research materials for each interview so that every child could feel free to express their feelings without finding the interview too intense or intrusive. Children's differing degrees of emotional resilience had to be taken into account too. Even siblings who were in contact with the same birth relative could exhibit very different attitudes, with one being deeply emotional about birth family issues while the other could appear to be almost indifferent.

CHAPTER 3

Preparation and Planning for Contact

Training and Preparation for Adopters and Foster Carers

All the families who participated in the study had access to training and preparation for adoption and fostering. All had one-to-one interviews with social workers and the majority also attended preparation groups. Contact with birth family was one important theme that was covered. Many families enthused about the quality of their preparation. They felt that the subject of contact was covered very thoroughly. Some families described their preparation for contact in glowing words such as 'excellent' 'first class' and 'perfect'. Some families who were initially hesitant about the concept of contact felt that their attitudes were transformed through debate within the group. A number stated that no amount of preparation could ever really prepare them for an event that would touch their lives at such a profound level.

Aspects of preparation that were particularly helpful were:
- The opportunity to think about contact from a child's perspective.
- Role-playing of different scenarios especially about the disruptive birth parent and thinking about personal attitudes and approaches to difficult situations.
- Open discussion with other adopters and foster carers and hearing first hand accounts about the grief processes associated with lack of contact from adopted adults and birth parents.

Some people felt that the following areas were not addressed adequately:
- The emotional aspect of contact was often addressed too superficially. Many families found the reality of contact much harder than they had anticipated. One adoptive mother summed up her experience with the phrase 'it was pretty bloody'.
- Preparing a child for contact and settling a child after contact.
- How to facilitate conflict resolution especially as there could be so many factions in any contact situation.

Although some people found that training transformed their attitudes others admitted that they had developed a psychological block because contact was too painful for them to handle.

It's a bit like being told that your child is disabled and you just block your mind to the reality.

Others stated frankly that they were prepared to feign agreement to the concept of contact because it was the only way that they could be sure that their application to adopt would be accepted.

> *I remember feeling I'll have to say 'Yes' to contact but when it comes to it I'll vote with my feet.*

At least one adopter talked about her resentment because she felt that her child was being treated like a guinea pig.

> *After the training course I felt quite cross. It's a bit like professionals promoting a 'wonder product' but there's no real guarantee about what it might do to you.*

Families with fostering experience had a real advantage over adopters. They had often worked with birth parents and had learned first hand how to manage the complexity of birth family situations. Others felt that their professional work experience played a part in equipping them to manage intricate relationships.

Changing attitudes

Sometimes there was a pivotal moment when adopters' perceptions about contact were radically transformed. For some this happened while debating the issues during training or preparation or while listening to a birth parent or an adoptee telling their personal story of grief and loss. Others changed their views as they reflected privately on the theme. One adopter found it helpful to consider the analogy of marriage.

> *When you're married you don't break links with your original family. Why do it for children?*

Another felt that the first lesson for any adoptive parent to learn must be to acknowledge that birth parenthood and adoption are not synonymous. When that had been achieved the concept of contact could be grasped.

> *Adoption isn't like having your own child. There's disappointment in that and you have to grieve the loss of your own child. Adoption is a different life path. It's more like a step-child or step-parent model. The child comes with a package. Adoption is like a parent and child living together rather than being closely bonded together. Once you accept that the life path is different it's easier to fit the idea of contact within it.*

Visual imagery helped others.

> *Adopted children have one foot in one circle and the other in another circle. The more you drive both feet apart the more unbalanced they become. The closer they come together the more balanced they become.*

Ethnicity and preparation for contact

Adopters and foster carers from minority ethnic and religious backgrounds highlighted the need for professionals to explore the complexity of contact issues with a sensitive attitude towards the applicant's cultural and religious beliefs. One Muslim social worker explained how it is possible to demonstrate to Muslim families that the concept of contact for a child is consistent with many teachings in the Koran. She felt that social workers often failed to invest time exploring these issues with families. She feared that a dire shortage of black and Asian families coming forward to adopt older children often resulted in social workers making the decision not to pursue contact plans for a child in case the family would withdraw. She advocated the use of professional interpreters to ensure that contact issues are adequately addressed and fully understood by applicants from minority ethnic backgrounds.

Personal life history: its profound influence on attitudes to contact

Although training played some role in shaping attitudes to contact, it was only minimally effective compared to the powerful influence of adopters and foster carers own personal experiences of broken family relationships. Of the 52 families interviewed 30 referred to personal experiences of loss throughout their own childhood. Such personal traumas inspired many families to put hours of energy into organising and maintaining significant contact relationships for children. These families had not derived their knowledge about contact through a textbook. They each had a personal story to relate that helped them to empathise with their child's sense of loss.

The personal experiences that adopters and foster carers felt were relevant included being adopted and having scant information about birth parents; a childhood spent in residential care or with bullying relatives; a breakdown in family relationships after the death of a sibling or parent; parental divorce resulting in the loss of a father; a traumatic separation from grandparents with no opportunity to say goodbye or to attend the funeral; observing a partner or relative suffer in adulthood because of a disrupted childhood. All spoke about the connection between these experiences and their determination to make contact a positive experience for their child.

There were positive and negative factors associated with families drawing on their own experiences. The positive aspects were that they could identify in a unique way with the adopted and foster child's sense of loss. Some had personal experience of fantasising about their absent birth parent and so they knew that their child was liable to have unrealistic expectations also.

I didn't see my dad from 7–25 years. I wondered whether my dad was someone rich? There were all these fairytales in my head. Was he famous? Was he rich? Was he a tramp? When I found him he was an ordinary working class man who had moved nowhere it was a shock. Because of my own experience my attitude was 'You must have contact'. I understood just how important it was.

Those who had chosen to sever a family relationship felt strongly about personal choice and were keen advocates of children's rights. Others who had observed disrupted family relationships being restored through keeping an 'open door' approach felt that a window of opportunity should always be there for the child. It is obvious why such adopters were so highly motivated to ensure that a contact relationship was retained even though it often triggered a lot of personal pain for them.

Some acknowledged with hindsight that it was very easy for their view of contact to be blinkered by their own experiences. In one particular case where disruption eventually occurred, the adopter recognised that she had not really listened carefully enough to the child's verbal and non-verbal protestations about seeing his birth mother, because her opinions had been driven by her own childhood experiences.

> *I was too set on contact because of my own childhood. I was adopted. I knew nothing of my family and I fantasised so much. I thought I was the illegitimate child of the Queen and Prince Philip. Because of my own childhood I felt contact was essential. When Andrew (10) was placed with us I kept thinking that had it been me, I would definitely have wanted contact with my birth mother. My views on contact have changed now. They're not so strong as they used to be.*

Another adopter sounded a note of caution and recognised the need for a balanced attitude.

> *You have to be careful not to make your own feelings the child's feelings.*

Meeting the Birth Relatives Prior to Contact

Meeting the birth parents prior to placement

Meeting one or more of the birth parents prior to the placement proved to be a useful preparation for placement. It was a highly significant event for many adopters. Thirty-three of the 76 families had the opportunity to do so. In some of these 33 cases this meeting was not associated with contact but rather arranged on a one-off basis usually because the birth parents or adopters requested it. This study echoed the findings of Fratter (1996) by evidencing that it was possible for these introductory meetings to be very constructive even when birth parents were not consenting to or actively opposing adoption. In some instances it resulted in formal consent to adoption being granted. The study material illustrated that there were both immediate and longer-term advantages in investing time in this meeting between the adults.

Meeting the birth parents prior to contact

Thirty-nine families had ongoing contact with one or both parents. An introductory meeting between the adults prior to contact had major advantages. These meetings provided an opportunity for adopters and foster carers to ask questions and to fill gaps in background information; they also provided fresh insights into the child's early life. One adoptive couple visited the birth mother's home. Seeing firsthand the squalor in which the birth mother lived was an eye opener. In an instant and without one word being spoken the prospective adopter could understand at a deep level why this mother could not provide for her children. Seven years after adoption she is still able to use this experience in a constructive way with her adopted children as she answers their questions about their origins. Another adoptive mother described how all her stereotyped ideas evaporated as she and the birth mother wept together.

> *I felt dreadful. I felt like a thief. It was a real turn around for me. I went to the meeting feeling resentful. I was blaming the birth mother and saying, 'How could any woman give up a child?' I could see that this mother really loved her daughter. I went away with a totally different view.*

Another adoptive family had their own private opinion about what alcoholic parents would be like. The adoptive father had grown up with an alcoholic father and so he was aware of the reality.

> *For us it helped de-mystify them as a couple. Our view of alcoholics was that they would be downtrodden. Instead they were upper middle class, well spoken and well behaved.*

Other families whose first meeting with birth parents coincided with the child's first contact meeting after placement, felt that they were seriously disadvantaged. Only one adoptive family regretted having had face-to-face dialogue with birth parents. In their case there had been no plans at the outset for face-to-face contact between Mark (10) and his birth parents. Mark pleaded again and again to see them. His birth parents also begged to see him. Professionals were opposed to this. After two years of Mark badgering his adoptive parents they promised him that they would fight to have his wish fulfilled. The adoptive mother admitted that she had never stopped feeling sorry for the birth parents since the first day she had met them and that this had blurred her vision of the dangers inherent in their situation. After Mark's first contact meeting with his birth parents his unsettled adoption placement began to deteriorate and then disrupted.

Meeting other birth relatives prior to contact

Introductory meetings between adopters or foster carers and other birth relatives were also very important. Sometimes these meetings were not feasible because the birth relative was hostile towards the placement. When such negative sentiments existed at the outset they were liable to impinge on ongoing contact relationships. Examples from this study illustrate that it was inadvisable for contact to proceed with a birth relative who refused to engage in this introductory meeting.

Preparation of Children for Contact

Ascertaining children's wishes and feelings about contact

This research study derived information from two sources, about whether children's wishes and feelings about contact had been ascertained at any stage leading up to their permanent placement or since placement:

- Interviews with adopters and foster carers.
- Interviews with children and young people.

Social workers who were interviewed about 29 placements where adopters and foster carers had failed to respond were not asked to comment on the degree to which they had attempted to ascertain children's wishes and feelings. As this social worker was usually responsible for direct work with the child it seemed unfair to expect her to express an objective viewpoint about her own professional practice. This important issue was therefore raised in interviews with adopters and foster carers and with children and young people themselves. It was therefore examined in relation to 77 placements, comprising 64 adoption placements and 13 fostering placements.

Did professionals ask children for their views about contact?

Ages of children at point of placement

0–5 years	5–11 years	11–18 years
10	51	16

Figure 9a: Age of children at point of placement

It is helpful to consider the question about whether children's views were ascertained, alongside information about the age of the 77 children at the point of placement (see Figure 9a).

Responses of adopters and foster carers

Yes	No	Child too disturbed and unsettled to express a view	Child too young to be asked	Child asked but viewpoint ignored
24	16	18	18	1
31%	21%	23%	23%	1%

Figure 9b: Responses of adopters and foster carers

What did adopters and foster carers think about professional attempts to ascertain children's wishes and feelings about contact? There were some excellent examples of professionals giving children a full opportunity to express their views about contact. Adopters and foster carers used phrases like, 'He was always fully consulted'; 'She was asked every step of the way'.

In some situations contact issues were fully explored with children through Life Story work. It was noticeable that the quality of social work practice received effusive praise when the social worker had known the child for a very long time.

> *The only word I can find to describe the social worker is 'brilliant'. She'd known Philip from three to eleven years old and she was so committed to him.*

There were also examples of very poor social work practice where the social worker failed to invest time with the child or just did not seem to have the ability to communicate at the child's level.

> *The social worker wasn't capable of talking to a child in a sensitive way. I was a bit shocked that she just did not seem to have the skills.*

Eighteen children were considered too young at the point of placement to have a viewpoint about contact. This was not always associated with the child's chronological age. Some children were considered old enough to engage in the process at five years especially when it was integrated into Life Story work while others at the age of eight years were described as 'too young to make any kind of conscious decision'.

Eighteen children were considered to be too disturbed to engage in any meaningful discussion about contact issues. Phrases were used like; 'There was too much trauma in her life and she lacked focus'; 'He was all over the place and couldn't sit still for five minutes'; 'They couldn't get their feelings across and they were so frightened'. This group of children were clearly already weighed down with a range of emotional problems and were having great difficulty making a transition to a new family. It was therefore very difficult for social workers to have a meaningful dialogue with them about their wishes in relation to contact with their birth relatives.

Andrew (10) did express his views about contact on every occasion that he was expected to travel to see his birth mother. His hysterical screams, violent temper tantrums and consistent protestations of, 'I don't want to see her, I want her dead' could last for hours. However, his social worker continued with the contact plan, insisting that Andrew 'was playing psychological games'. Later Andrew's placement disrupted and he was placed in a Secure Unit. An independent psychological assessment stated:

> *The birth mother was passing sexual signals to Andrew during contact. He was deeply distressed and intimidated by being near her. Contact should have been terminated at a much earlier stage because of the level of sexual feeling that it was stirring for the child.*

Children's responses

Thirty-seven children and young people who participated in the study were asked the question:

Yes	No	Asked a little but not enough	Too young to be asked
14	10	7	6
38%	27%	19%	16%

Figure 9c: Children's responses

Did anyone ask you who you would like to keep in contact with from your birth family?

Fourteen children expressed satisfaction about the fact that they had been asked about contact. 'I was asked lots' was a phrase that was used by several children. Tricia (11) liked the fact that so many people sought her opinion:

I wasn't just asked by one person. My social worker asked, my social worker's boss asked and my therapist asked me too.

Fahad (12) added the following advice:

It's good to be asked a number of times because the situation can change.

Ten children complained that their viewpoint had not been taken into consideration. Marian joined her adoptive family when she was six years old. She complained bitterly that she had never been asked whether she wanted to live on her own or with her brothers. As far as she was concerned seeing her brothers regularly at contact meetings was not the same as living with them. After being four years in her placement on her own she still resented her social worker for not being prepared to listen to her. Donna (12) said that she felt cheated. Contact with her birth father had been established when he had requested it but the family member whom she really wanted to see was her birth mother. She had lived with her birth mother until she was eight years old. She had never known her birth father because the relationship between her birth parents had been so transient, lasting merely a few weeks. This is how her adoptive mother described Donna's relationship with her birth father.

She doesn't know him. She has no affection for him. She thinks he's boring. He doesn't know how to talk to her. He carries a photograph in his wallet of a cute attractive child – his daughter. If she's going to keep contact when she's 15–16 he has to put more effort into it. He talks about himself all the time. He tells her that he's putting an extension on his house. She's not really interested.

Kim was nine when she joined her adoptive family. She sees her birth mother annually. She complained that there were several other important birth relatives with whom she yearned to retain contact but her social worker had not stopped to listen to her viewpoint. Tears flowed as she explained that Auntie B had now died and that she had not been allowed to say Goodbye.

Seven children said that although there had been some dialogue with them about contact they wanted to be consulted more. Jill (11) needed extra time spent with her because of her special needs. It was insufficient for her to be asked once by her social worker for her opinion. She required a much greater investment of time. She took a long time to articulate her views during the research interview but she made one point very clearly.

My social worker asked me sometimes but not enough.

Other children said that they felt that they should have been consulted more about the following issues:

- The frequency.
- The length of time it lasted.
- The venue.
- The kind of activity they engaged in.

One child felt aggrieved because his social worker never asked him if he would like to continue to see Spotty, his pet dog. He was five years old when he joined his new family. His birth parents had been chronic alcoholics and they had left him for two nights unattended. During these nights his dog was lying by his side. His dog was extra special because she had saved his life and he was worried that she would be maltreated.

Ascertaining children's wishes and feelings: significant differences between adoption and fostering placements

The question of whether children were consulted or not about contact did not appear to be associated with whether the placement was fostering or adoption. Irrespective of the type of placement much depended on the social worker having time to invest with the child, and appropriate skills to communicate effectively with the child.

One factor that was significantly different in fostering placements was that children had much greater opportunity to have an ongoing dialogue with their social worker as their placement stretched over many years. This was especially significant because some children's level of instability at the beginning of their placement was too high for them to be able to contribute fully in the formulation of contact plans. Foster children also had access to a Review system where contact plans could be re-evaluated and amended. In contrast, children who had been legally adopted did not have easy access to any professional forum where they could re-state their views about contact. Naturally some did talk to their adoptive parents. However, the adoptive parents were frequently powerless to create change in or to instigate a new contact plan. Several adopters who consulted social services many years after adoption when there was a need to change the contact arrangements were deeply disappointed. They quickly discovered that the initial enthusiasm that social workers had expressed about the theoretical concept of contact during their preparation and assessment period did not extend to a long term practical commitment to implement essential changes in contact arrangements that reflected the child's best interests.

Preparing to say Goodbye to significant birth family members

Saying Goodbye to significant birth family members was not an issue that was raised in the interview questionnaire. However, a number of families wanted to talk about this theme because it had been difficult for them.

Four families talked about social workers arranging a contact visit for their child with neither the child nor the adopters being aware that this was intended to be a final farewell. It was only later that this became apparent. Some children were devastated to discover that they would be unable to see their birth relative again. At the point of participation in this study some children were clearly still trying to come to terms with the abrupt severance of such crucial relationships. One 11-year-old girl, who had been unaware that her last meeting with her birth mother was a Goodbye visit, said that she had been under the impression, for several years after joining her adoptive family, that her adopters had 'stolen' her.

Anita was nine years old when she was placed with her adoptive family. One year after joining her new family her social worker took her to see her previous foster family and her younger brother who was in foster care. Anita was excited about going on a trip with her social worker and getting sweets. Her adoptive parents were struggling with her placement and welcomed some respite from Anita's demands. As her adoptive parents described Anita's situation it became apparent that they were unsure about whether this visit to her brother was intended to be a final visit. They had a vague idea that they were supposed to instigate further meetings if Anita asked for this. She never did but this was not surprising. During the early months with them Anita had displayed a lot of emotion about her birth mother and had wanted to purchase some special gifts for her, but as her adopters had failed to respond she had gradually closed down all emotional response. Anita's adoptive father was clear about his attitude to contact. He felt that it was likely to be detrimental to any child because it re-opened old wounds. How could this family respond sensitively to Anita's complex feelings and wishes about her birth family?

Elaine was six years old when she joined her adoptive family. Her social worker felt that it would be a good idea if she prepared a farewell tape for her birth mother. This would be one way for Elaine to come to terms with the reality of what was happening and the tape would be a special souvenir for her birth mother to cherish. As soon as Elaine joined her adoptive family her level of grief about broken bonds with her birth mother surfaced.

*During the first few months of the placement Elaine was heartbroken.
She'd sob and sob because she couldn't see her mother or sister
anymore. She kept asking, 'Why can't I see them?' My mum might die'.
We felt that it was wrong to stop contact. Elaine had lots of memories,
both good and bad.*

Eventually Elaine's adoptive parents persuaded professionals that a
contact plan was essential. Now, six years later that plan is still ongoing.
Elaine still recoils in horror as she remembers the trauma associated with
being forced to record words on her social worker's tape recorder that were
diametrically opposed to what she truly felt.

*Her birth mother still says that the tape was so terrible and cruel. Elaine
still fights back her tears and says, 'They made me make that tape and
told me what to say'. Since adoption she's sent tapes to her birth mother.
They're very spontaneous. She just sits and talks into the tape. 'Now
I'm going to sing you a song'. She says that she does it to make up for
the first tape.*

Life Story work: an important tool in the preparation of children for contact

When good quality Life Story work was undertaken with a child, an important
foundation was laid through which children could gain a clear view about
their family relationships and begin to grapple with the complex emotions
associated with abuse. It was vital that children understood their family
situation. If they did not there was a danger that their understanding of
face-to-face contact could become very confused and their expectations
quite unrealistic.

Some field and residential social workers had invested many hours
compiling Life Story Books with children. This was time well spent. An
attractively presented and carefully prepared Life Story Book was an
effective way of valuing a child's past. In contrast some children had Life
Story Books that had been prepared in rather a slovenly manner. Some
remained unfinished because the social worker who had instigated the work
had been transferred to another post. Others were given to the adoptive
parents in an incomplete form with the intention that they might add to the
child's story.

Two adoptive mothers had made exceptional use of Life Story work. They
were both teachers with special expertise in working with children. One had
created a range of allegorical story-books that enabled the child to
understand the meaning of adoption. The other simply added to the Life
Story Book each time Pete (9) became uncontrollably angry. When an
explosive temper tantrum had subsided the adoptive mother would take Pete
on her knee and encourage him to talk about his anger and distress.

Together they then recorded his memories about his birth family on the computer and incorporated a printed copy in a loose-leaf folder in the Life Story Book. This was a demonstration to Pete about how important his feelings were.

'Why don't I live with my sibling?'

Decisions about splitting siblings are often made by professionals after an agonising debate. Of course the decision not to place siblings in the same family does not mean that all contact has to be severed. In fact it is common for links to be retained. This study illustrates how important it is that the children grasp the reasons for splitting and are able to work through their feelings about it. Reasons for splitting may be about one child's sexualised, aggressive or dominant behaviour or about the needs of one child overpowering and eclipsing the other. Splitting may also be necessary because it may be unrealistic to expect the prospective adoptive family to cope with the competing and excessive demands of deeply deprived children. It is not easy to explain these adult concepts in a child-friendly way. If these explanations are not undertaken children's anger about splitting is liable to spill over into contact meetings and seriously impede a potentially positive contact arrangement. There is one vivid example of this in the study. Noel was seven when he was placed with his adoptive family. He had one brother with special needs to whom he was exceptionally close. Both had been severely beaten in their birth family and could remember their joint admissions to hospital. Moving to foster care had not been easy but at least both boys had been able to live together. After two years in foster care the strain on the foster family escalated and they asked for Noel to be removed. Noel's inability to grasp why he was separated from his brother has made contact meetings between the boys almost unmanageable. Noel's adoptive mother knows that these issues have at times brought the placement close to disruption. She has strong feelings about the need for professionals to explain decisions about splitting directly to children.

> *I feel that someone needs to explain to Noel who made these decisions about moving him on from the foster home while his brother remained. He needs to understand, why, what and how? I get all Noel's flack. His previous foster mother gets all his flack when he goes to see his brother. He doesn't understand why his brother was 'chosen' and not he. Noel lives through horrendous moods and rages. The after-effects associated with contact are dreadful. You can sense his sadness and loss.*

Countdown to the contact meeting

How much notice should a child have of the fact that a contact meeting is pending? This did not seem to depend on the child's chronological age but rather on the child's capacity to handle the tension associated with waiting for the event. Some children could not cope with knowing anything in advance. Ryan (12) and Perry (11) have been six years with their foster family. Although they did enjoy some aspects of contact with their birth father they were unable to tolerate the anxiety engendered by waiting. Their foster father has learned from experience that it is beneficial to inform them immediately prior to the event and to use the travelling time for preparation and discussion.

> *When I prepared them days before there were more problems. It was better to catch them unawares and just say 'We're off' and then talk. They still get apprehensive.*

Other families found that the best strategy was to give the child at least two weeks notice and to go through the routine of marking off the dates on a calendar. Even some very young children benefited from this approach.

> *With Keith (5) we count down the number of night sleeps before he'll see his birth father.*

There were a group of children in the study who had a particular problem when their daily routines were disturbed. They were often children who had been diagnosed as suffering from Attention Deficit and Hyperactivity Disorder (ADHD). There was obviously a sense of security associated with having a clearly defined and predictable routine. Any deviation from the norm disturbed the child's equilibrium. One adopter described her five-year-old girl as hysterical when contact disturbed the regular pattern of her day. Another said:

> *You can't surprise her or it will destroy her.*

Adopters and foster carers had to do the most painstaking preparation for children in this group, often writing down a detailed plan and even role playing it several times with the child prior to the contact visit. Several children had their own mobile telephone. There were examples in this study of children contacting their siblings by mobile telephone with deeply disturbing effects. Some siblings just could not cope with this sudden and highly emotive interruption to their organised daily routine. Jonathan (10), who had been diagnosed with ADHD made a serious suicide attempt following a totally unexpected mobile telephone call from his sister whom he had not seen for two years.

Questions that a child might need answered prior to face-to-face contact

Natasha (7) and Paula (3) are sisters. Natasha lived with her birth mother until she was four years old but Paula was removed from the family at birth. Diverse experiences in the birth family resulted in the girl's feelings towards their birth mother being markedly different. Paula appeared to have no interest in her birth mother but Natasha was deeply concerned that contact with her birth mother might be severed. She felt aggrieved because the contact plan stated that she could only see her birth mother once a year. Although Natasha really wanted to see her birth mother she was also very anxious about meeting her. The questions with which Natasha bombarded her adoptive mother provide a glimpse into the kind of questions to which a child might need answers, prior to face-to-face contact.

- Will my real mum know where I live?
- Who will be there?
- How long will the meeting last?
- Who will I sit next to?
- Can I have my real mum on one side and you on the other?
- What happens if I don't want to stay?
- What if you and my real mum have a fight during the meeting?
- What if my real mum doesn't want me to come back here?
- How will I say Good-bye?

Management of behaviour problems prior to contact meetings

In general, the behaviour exhibited by children prior to contact was less intense than the aftermath. Anxiety, regression, nervousness, extreme introversion and a detachment from reality were signs that adopters and foster carers observed in children when they knew that a contact meeting was pending. Some children openly rejected their adoptive parents in the days leading up to contact. In a minority of cases children's behaviour escalated out of control. One eight-year-old boy soiled and smeared and slept with a baseball bat by his bedside in case his birth parents abducted him. Another teenager became deeply disturbed.

All the signs were that he was deeply agitated. He'd go on and on in an obsessive way about violent scenes from videos: about blood and about people being splatted.

Marian (6) wanted to tell the whole world that she was seeing her birth family. She told the milkman, her teacher, and her adoptive mother's close friends and relatives. This could be a painful experience for her adoptive mother who at a deep level yearned to have an exclusive claim on her child.

Preparing the child for displays of grief from their birth relative

Some adopters felt that it was important to explain to the child that their birth relative might dissolve into tears. This was important because some birth relatives were not able to control their emotions. Some wept openly in front of the child. Mary was five and her younger brother Craig was four when they joined their adoptive family. Their grandparents had fought for custody of

them following incidents of non-accidental injury in their birth family. Mary
and Craig had lived with their grandparents until their grandmother died.
Their first contact meeting with their grandfather was heart rending for
everyone.

> *Grandfather came to the house. He was very tearful. He's had two*
> *bereavements. He's lost his wife and he's lost his grandchildren. The*
> *first night he spent in a Guest House and he had agreed to visit the*
> *children again the next day. He came back the next day and put money*
> *on the table to buy slippers for the children. He said that he didn't want*
> *to see the children. He just couldn't cope.*

After a period of recovery over a number of months and counselling and
support provided by his social worker, grandfather has been able to work
through these traumatic losses. He now sees the children four times annually.
This has grown into one of the happiest contact relationships that emerged
in this study.

Developing routines as a preparation for contact

Some families developed rituals and routines in the days leading up to
contact that helped prepare children in a very natural way for contact
meetings. One family always baked a special cake. Others made home-
made gifts or the children drew pictures. Children enjoyed these special
times and it was natural to discuss sensitive issues surrounding the birth
family while making these practical preparations.

Devising alternative plans

Some families described how plans for contact always included an additional
plan that they kept up their sleeve. Ryan is now 12 years old and his younger
brother Perry is 11 years. They see their birth father several times annually.
Their birth father has a criminal record and has spent considerable
periods of his life in prison. These contact meetings always involve some
kind of activity for the boys but it is easy for emotions to escalate out of
control. Ryan and Perry's foster father offered this advice.

> *Have alternatives planned at all times. It can change the whole scenario.*
> *If the boys are doing art and almost fighting I say, 'Lets have a game of*
> *football' or, 'Let's go down to the beach'. Changing the activity will*
> *immediately dissipate the tension.*

Planning a special activity after contact

Another simple tactic that worked well was when families planned to do
something special immediately following contact, like visiting MacDonalds,
shopping for something special, making the child's favourite food for Sunday
lunch, or going to a sporting activity that the child would enjoy.

Choosing the Right Venue

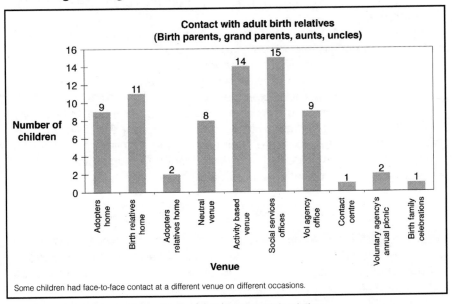

Some children had face-to-face contact at a different venue on different occasions.

Figure 10: Contact with adult birth relatives

Neutral venue	Activity based venue
Sainsbury's car park	Bowling
Shopping centre	Swimming
Museum	Art
Restaurant	Ceramic painting
Railway station	Football
Family pub	Leisure centre

Figure 10 indicates which venue was used for contact meetings with adult birth relatives such as birth parents, grandparents, aunts and uncles. Information about the venue used for sibling contact is detailed in Chapter 6. Contact meetings needed to occur in a relaxed setting, with child-centred activities and adequate supervision but many families expressed disappointment because of a dearth of such suitable venues. A considerable number who decided to use their own home or a birth relative's home quickly discovered that there were disadvantages associated with doing so and they were eager to advise others to begin contact meetings at a neutral venue.

Some families felt angry because their social worker's recommendation about a contact venue was totally inappropriate.

The social worker suggested The Imperial War Museum. We decided that if she kept insisting that we were not going to go. I got the Guide

*Book to London and read this, 'It recreates the sounds and smells of
trench warfare'. For children who were frightened of the dark it wasn't
appropriate.*

Another family felt angry because their social worker suggested that a
contact meeting could happen at Waterloo station.

*It has to be a quality venue. The children need to meet in a good
environment. The back of cafés in railway stations is not suitable. It has
to be private, clean, warm and welcoming.*

A useful parallel can be drawn here. An attractive good quality Life Story
Book, rather than a ragged scrap book conveys a message to children about
their value and the significance of their early history. Similarly a high-quality
contact venue speaks volumes to children about how much importance
adults attribute to their relationship with a birth relative.

The advantages and disadvantages of using the adopters' home

It was very easy for adopters to agree to contact meetings occurring in their
own home without stopping to reflect on the implications of this. However,
this study indicates that some of the advantages associated with using this
type of resource were short term and immediate rather than longer term. One
special advantage was that the adopted and foster children were themselves
relaxed and comfortable in their own familiar environment. An air of
informality eased tension for everyone.

It was often after several years of using this contact venue that the real
disadvantages became evident. The most worrying issue concerned the loss
of anonymity for the child and the adopters. The lives of the birth families that
featured in this study were marked by instability. Many birth parents had split
up in the most acrimonious of circumstances. Sometimes one birth parent
had been granted face-to-face contact with a child with the clear understanding that they would not divulge the child's whereabouts to an
ex-partner. In the longer term some of these severed adult relationships were
rekindled. These were often very immature short-lived relationships but in the
excitement of finding love again some birth parents breached their firm
promise not to disclose the child's whereabouts. Some of those birth parents
that had been banned from having contact with their child were Schedule 1
Offenders. The risks associated with this type of situation were high. Some
adopters were seriously concerned about the safety of their child at the time
they participated in this research study.

When choosing the contact venue it was vitally important to assess the
potential risks associated with the loss of anonymity. Kevin (9) Lyn (8) and
Rikki (6) were placed for adoption together. Their maternal grandfather loved
them and wanted to keep in contact with them. At the time of placement their
birth mother could not be found. Grandfather's girlfriend played a prominent

part in these contact meetings but when differences of opinion arose between her and the adopters their harmonious relationship evaporated and contact meetings were severed. The fact that the birth mother has now decided to return to her home village has created current concerns for the adopters. The adoptive mother is worried about the possibility of grandfather telling the birth mother where the children live. However much the adoptive mother wants to protect her children this is a matter that is totally beyond her control.

If the birth mother managed to get my name and address from granddad she could turn up on the doorstep. If I shut the door in her face the children might hear the conflict. If I rang the police I don't really think they'd want to know. Would they even come out? You need to be on your guard and ready and able to take precautions.

Another single foster carer felt angry because her social worker had placed her under undue pressure to agree to use her home as the venue for contact with the birth father despite the fact that on several occasions he had made sexual overtures towards her.

The advantages and disadvantages of using the birth relative's home

Mark (8) was brought up by alcoholic birth parents. During his time in foster care his grandmother wrote to him and phoned him regularly. He also spent one week with her during school breaks. When he was placed for adoption this pattern of contact with his grandmother during school holidays was retained. The arrangement worked well for everyone. However this case was exceptional. Usually there were difficulties when contact occurred in the birth relative's home or in the geographical area where the birth relatives lived.

Elaine was six when she joined her adoptive family while Katie her older sister remained with her birth mother. One major issue that has always perplexed Elaine is why her birth mother kept her sister and allowed her to be adopted. Although it had not been part of the plan that face-to-face contact would happen at the birth mother's house this happened almost by accident one day when it was raining and the birth mother suggested that they could go to her house. Caught unawares, Elaine's adoptive mother was not sure how to decline this invitation. She quickly discovered that it raised particular difficulties for Elaine.

It's been very personal for Elaine going to the house. She sees Katie's bedroom and she thinks, 'That should be me sleeping there.'

On another occasion when Elaine and her adoptive parents had driven Katie back to her birth mother's house a more serious incident occurred.

Elaine went in first. Her face dropped as she saw the back of a figure disappearing upstairs. Elaine whispered to me, 'It's Tom' (a previous partner of the birth mother). He had been violent. Elaine remembered him having a knife, the police being called and she was very frightened. She had told us previously that Tom had held a knife to her throat. (After the adoption we read about him in her background notes. It said that Tom had been imprisoned for drugs and that he had escaped from prison. The birth mother had to be re-housed to avoid danger.) We sat in the living room. The birth mother said to Elaine, 'You remember Tom. Don't you want to see him?' Elaine was very upset.

When contact occurred in the birth family's home it gave back a degree of power to the birth family. Sometimes this was not in the child's best interests.

Keith joined his adoptive family when he was 11 years old. Contact with his birth father occurred either in his birth father's home or in an aunt's house. At one point the pressure exerted on Keith by his birth father to change the adoption plan to fostering brought the placement close to disruption.

Activity based contact

A contact meeting that was established around some type of enjoyable activity for the child often worked well. As Figure 10 indicates, a wide range of activities were used. It was important to consider whether the activity was right in relation to the degree of supervision that was required. For example, one adopter described the disadvantages of bowling. When it was the adoptive mother's turn to bowl the birth mother would capitalise on this moment of distraction and begin to interrogate the child. Another single adopter described how uncomfortable she felt in a restaurant with the birth father. Sitting opposite him was a very intense experience as he focused all his attention on her rather than on the child. One family recommended using the viewing area of an international airport. There was space for the children to run around, distractions through the airport activity and yet sufficient privacy when they needed to find a quiet corner for personal dialogue.

Annual events

Some voluntary agencies and one social services department had a specialist annual event such as a picnic or a Christmas party for adoptive families. This was an excellent place for contact to occur for some children with adequate informal social work supervision and plenty of distractions. It was ideal for children who only had annual contact and merely wanted to see a birth relative for a few minutes and then run away to play. Anonymity and confidentiality were protected. Even if contact was difficult the child could enjoy lots of fun activities that staff had organised for this special day.

Specialist contact centres

Specialist contact centres were rarely available. One family was effusive in their praise for Coram Contact Centre.

I liked the neutral venue. It was comfortable, friendly and like someone's flat. It was a bit like a normal house with age appropriate games and activities. The staff didn't give you a sense of being judged.

There was a very strong plea from many families for this type of resource to be more widely available in different geographical areas in Britain.

Written Contact Agreements

All the families did receive some written information about contact plans either through these plans being detailed on Form E, through minutes of planning or review meetings or through correspondence from social services or their voluntary agency. Form E, originally prepared by British Agencies for Adoption and Fostering (BAAF) is used by agencies as a way of collating full background information about children requiring adoptive or foster families.

Formal contact agreements in adoption

In the SSI 1995 study *Moving The Goalposts*, they state that contact agreements are invaluable and should become standard practice:

> *The existence of a written agreement helps to prevent confusion not only between the various parties to adoption, but within the agency itself.*

Despite this recommendation, formal written contact agreements were only used in relation to as few as 20 out of 86 adoption placements. In a further ten cases, attempts were made to establish a contact agreement but these documents were not finalised, either because one party to the agreement refused consent or because a social services social worker failed to complete the necessary documentation. However, there were noticeable signs that written agreements were becoming more common in recent placements.

Reasons for incomplete contact agreements

Birth father refused consent	Birth mother refused consent	Child refused consent	Social service's failure to complete documentation
4	1	1	4

Figure 11: Reasons for incomplete contact agreements

In situations where social services failed to undertake their responsibilities for written agreements the original social worker had usually left and months of delay ensued. One social worker from a voluntary agency expressed exasperation about such poor professional practice which she knew had left one adoptive family completely disillusioned.

Social services have been incredibly bad. The social worker has changed so many times. Each time we try to discuss it we're talking to a new social worker who asks for time to read the case file and settle into the new job.

Another social worker who had encountered similar frustrations commented:

Just trying to get Social services to write a ten-line contact agreement is totally impossible.

At what stage of placement should contact agreements be prepared?

Some families complained bitterly that contact agreements were not devised at an early enough phase of the placement. It was not unusual for agreements to be issued several years after adoption. Some social workers seemed to assume that the contact plan had to be fully tested out before it reached the stage of a signed formal agreement. This had serious implications for a child like Natasha (10). Contact with the birth mother had been vitally important for her. Her social services social worker transferred to a new post and the contact plan drifted. It proved very difficult to reassure Natasha that her wish to see her birth mother would be fulfilled especially as no written agreement existed. Natasha had often been let down by adults in the past. Suddenly she began to fear that all the verbal promises made by social workers might be a lie. At night she lay awake fretting about whether her adoption would ever be realised. During the day her anxiety level reached fever pitch and threatened to de-stabilise her placement.

The study indicates that a better route forward for contact agreements was to draft a tentative agreement early in the placement with the clear understanding that change is likely to be required as the plan becomes a reality. The most sophisticated contact agreement in this study concerned a sibling placement of three boys, Richard, Jason and Liam who were nine, eight and six at placement. Contact is maintained with the birth mother and two older sisters, one of whom lives in a Refuge and the other in a leaving-care flat. One factor that has enabled these boys to maintain contact with their complex birth family for four years has been the imaginative and dynamic use of a contact agreement to which all the parties have contributed. Both social services and the voluntary agency are committed to contact in this case and both are involved in supervising and supporting it. The contact agreement requires that the birth family undergo counselling immediately prior to contact to ensure that they are emotionally attuned to the boys needs. As difficulties have arisen during contact new issues have been added to the agreement. Each party has been able to raise issues that have upset them. Examples of themes that have been added include appropriate physical contact, confidentiality for the boys, banning secrets and whispering during contact meetings. This case demonstrates how a contact agreement can be used creatively, ensuring that regular review occurs and that adequate support is available for all parties.

Content of contact agreements

Social workers and adopters talked about the importance of designing contact agreements that were specific and practical. The following framework for a contact agreement is based on the experiences and recommendations of adopters and social workers.

General issues to be addressed in all contact agreements	Examples of specific issues that may need to be addressed
Purpose of contact. Who attends? Venue: where contact happens? Frequency of contact. Timing and structure of contact. Confidentiality. How people are to be addressed and names to be used during meetings. Areas of conversation to be avoided, e.g. denying reasons why the child could not live with birth parents: inappropriate descriptions of lurid details about events occurring in the birth family. Supervision arrangements. Policy re exchanging gifts. System for reviewing and if necessary changing the contact plan. Support system for all parties and how it can be accessed. Complaints system.	Ground rules about use of language (e.g. sexually explicit language, swearing). Use of false promises or inappropriate interrogation of the child. Secrecy, whispering. Managing physical contact when meeting and parting. Punctuality.

A minority view

A minority of families stated that a written contact agreement made them feel too restrained. The SSI 1995 study *Moving The Goalposts* emphasised the importance of negotiation between social services and adopters when devising a contact agreement.

> *The negotiating process required to establish an agreement is a necessary and helpful one, and can play a major role in reducing and removing conflict.*

When this process was missing adopters often felt completely disempowered. One single adopter who had spent a lot of time in dispute with social services about contact plans did not feel that her viewpoint was considered. Consequently she perceived a contact agreement as an intrusion into her life. The fact that there was no agreed system for reviewing contact plans compounded her dissatisfaction.

> *I eventually got it written down. I found that unhelpful. It made me feel that it was set. It felt too rigid. It felt like they didn't trust me because it was written down. The way they write it is quite legal.*

The views of children and young people about formal contact agreements

What did the children and young people who participated in the study think about contact agreements? Thirty-seven children and young people participated in the study. The question of written agreements was addressed with 22 children who were 12 years and upwards. Twelve said that they were not aware that their contact plan had been written. Six expressed indifference about this and stated that the most important thing was that they were asked about it and that their views were incorporated into the plan. Another six said that they felt that it should be written because:

> *Writing is more official and you know that it is definitely happening.*

Ten children did recollect that the contact plan had been committed to writing. Brendan (15) felt devastated because his birth mother had said 'No' when she was asked if she wanted to see him. After six years of contact his birth father had lost interest in seeing him. Brendan's adoptive mother described him as 'constantly angry'. He resented the fact that his social services social worker had been so inept and that the written contact plan had never really been shared with him. With an air of disdain he stated:

> *I suppose writing it down would remind a few sleepy social workers.*

Regina (14) had been in an adoption placement that had disrupted. By the time she participated in this study she had found a new permanent foster family. She had ambivalent feelings about contact with her birth father. She was unsure about having the contact plan written because she felt pressurised by it.

> *I'm at a stage when social workers don't rule my life. It feels a bit like that if it's written.*

Debra (18) was an extrovert who had put endless energy into the task of keeping in contact with her large birth family. She had learned through experience that a good written agreement does not necessarily guarantee that a contact relationship will be problem free.

A contract was drawn up with my birth dad but he kept breaking it. One minute he'd agree but then he kept mucking it up.

Sam (14) was deeply attached to his younger brother who had remained in the care of his birth mother. He had written to the authorities to complain because his birth mother had banned his brother from seeing him. He felt that a written plan for contact was vital and that his birth mother should have been forced to sign an agreement.

Fahad (14) proposed the view that all children from the age of 11 years should be asked to sign a contact agreement. He felt that prior to that age he would not have been prepared to listen.

Chloe (17) had suffered abuse within her birth family and extended family. During her five year adoption placement she had been able to retain contact with her four siblings. Due to her abusive past it was essential to place firm boundaries around each of her family relationships. At times Chloe had rebelled and resented these restrictions. With hindsight she could see the value of having had a written agreement. She was now looking forward to the relaxation of some of these rules.

It was a good idea to have it written at the beginning. Questions like, when, where, how long? are important. Now that we're all grown up we can arrange it ourselves. For 17 years of my life I've never had a member of my birth family here on my birthday. My sister's 21st is coming up. She's invited all the family. It'll be an all-night do. We'll all go. It'll be the first time that we've all gone to a big family party. It'll be cool.

While children and young people expressed a range of different opinions about the value of having written contact agreements, it was obvious that this was not a topic to which they attributed great importance. A much more vital aspect that emerged again and again during research interviews was that children wanted social workers to spend time listening carefully to their opinions and ensuring that their wishes were taken into account. Such matters were undoubtedly of primary importance. Whether the plan was committed to writing was of secondary importance and for some children it really did not matter at all.

Summary of Key Points

- The majority of adopters and foster carers valued the training and preparation provided about contact by agencies. However, most found the real experience of contact and the feelings engendered by it more difficult than they had anticipated.
- Personal trauma associated with broken family relationships in adopters' and foster carers' own childhoods is liable to influence their view of contact. It is important that these issues are discussed during the assessment period so that those unresolved losses and unfulfilled hopes do not intrude unhelpfully into the child's contact plan.
- Foster carers and adopters of minority ethnic and religious backgrounds are likely to identify more fully with the complexity of contact issues if they are set within the familiarity of their own beliefs and values.
- It is essential to establish an introductory meeting between the adopters or foster carers and birth relatives prior to the first contact meeting. If a birth relative is unwilling to engage in this initial meeting there is a serious risk that this negative attitude will influence ongoing contact plans.
- Children need to grasp the reasons why professionals may have decided to split them from a sibling. Reasons for splitting may be complex and difficult to translate into a child's language. If this groundwork is not undertaken there are liable to be adverse implications for ongoing sibling contact.
- Life Story work is an excellent way of discussing sensitive issues surrounding contact with children. It also provides a medium through which children can give expression to their wishes and feelings about contact.
- Goodbye visits to birth relatives prior to placement need to be carefully explained to a child so that the child does not retain unrealistic hopes about contact.
- Adopted and foster children need to have opportunities to voice their opinions and feelings about contact not only prior to the placement but also as the placement becomes more established and significant changes in the contact plan may be required. Foster children can do this through the review system. Adopted children have no established forum where their ongoing opinions about contact can be heard.
- When choosing a contact venue it is important to consider whether using the adopter's home or the geographical location where the birth family live may jeopardise the child's safety. It is especially important to undertake a risk analysis of the current and potential links between

the birth relative who is maintaining contact and other individuals who have perpetrated abuse. Will confidentiality and anonymity be adequately protected not only at the present time but also in the long-term future?

- Formal written contact agreements are an important way of ensuring that contact plans have clear boundaries and that the safety of a child is addressed. A draft contact agreement needs to be prepared at the outset of the placement. Changes can occur later.
- Written contact agreements need to be specific and practical. A review system needs to exist whereby changes can be agreed and implemented.

CHAPTER 4

Approaching the Reality of Face-to-Face Contact

This chapter focuses on contact with adult relatives such as birth parents and grandparents, uncles and aunts. Chapter 6 addresses issues relevant to sibling contact.

Timing of the First Contact Meeting Following Placement

How soon after placement should the first contact with birth relatives occur? Obviously this needed to be worked out on an individual basis for each child. Occasionally the first contact occurred just weeks after placement but it was more common for a few months to elapse. In situations where birth relatives approved of the placement, a contact meeting weeks into placement could be quite a reassuring experience for the child. Kevin (9), Lynne (8) and Rikki (6) found their grandfather's visit exciting just four weeks after they joined their new family because he made no secret of the fact that he liked their new family. He expressed his good wishes by sending them all a good luck card.

When the decision was made that a child should be placed permanently with a family, there was a danger of changing the contact pattern too abruptly. Although professionals were aware why these sudden alterations occurred, children could be left bewildered. The most vivid example concerned a boy with severe learning difficulties who featured in the pilot study. David was 10 years old at placement. Prior to his adoption placement he had lived in residential care and been visited regularly by his grandmother, mother and sister. When he joined his adoptive family all birth relative contact was terminated. David could not verbalise his thoughts about family contact and professionals assumed that he would scarcely notice if his birth relatives disappeared out of his life. His adopters soon discovered differently.

David cried for his nanny, sister and his mum for a year. He went through a real bereavement. Every day he'd say, 'Get in car. Go and see nan'. We had a car so he couldn't understand why we weren't going.

This family eventually decided to defy professional advice and arrange a contact meeting. David was thrilled. Although he had not seen his birth family for more than a year, recollections of his animated facial expression remain imprinted on his adoptive parent's mind.

When birth relatives disapproved of the placement it was essential to give the child time to put down roots in the new family before arranging a contact meeting. Helen (12) had only been one week in her adoption placement when a face-to-face meeting with her birth mother was arranged. Her birth mother disapproved of the adoption plan. Despite the fact that contact was supervised the birth mother managed to pass a secret note to Helen with her mobile telephone number. A few days later when Helen had a minor disagreement with her adoptive mother she stormed out of the house. Later she was found at her birth mother's house. She adamantly refused to return to her adoptive family. At the disruption meeting Helen's adopter offered the following advice.

> *Regardless of how much Helen asked for contact, it shouldn't have happened for at least three months. She should have been told, 'If your relationship with your adopter is going to work it'll mean no contact with your birth mother for three months. She should have been told, 'This is an important relationship. It's important enough to put contact with your birth mother on hold'. She didn't get that message.*

However, there were disadvantages in delaying contact for too long also. Natasha (7) fretted for her birth mother. She had acted as a quasi-parent to her. She needed the reassurance of seeing for herself that her birth mother was well. When the plan for contact was deferred from six to nine months because her social worker had resigned from her post, she could not settle. As her adopter explained, 'Nine months is a long time in the life of a damaged seven-year-old'.

Sometimes plans for contact were accelerated or delayed to coincide with the child's birthday or Christmas. Several families discovered through experience that there were real disadvantages in arranging contact on these special days. The subject of gifts was an emotive one. Some birth parents just could not afford gifts yet they felt morally obliged to purchase them. One or two families actually stole the gifts that they provided. Some children felt guilt ridden about birth parents spending their scant income on a gift. Other children treated a gift from a birth parent with complete disdain.

> *Sean (8) wanted a Scalextric. His birth father bought him a huge one for his birthday costing nearly £100 (much more than we'd spend). Sean was unimpressed. He saw it as his birth father trying to buy his affection. He wouldn't play with it for a year. Some time later his adoptive grandpa bought him a set for £5 in a sale. That was quite acceptable and he loved playing with it.*

Another single adopter found that Christmas was too emotive a time for contact to occur. It simply added to the intensity and instability of the placement.

> *Contact happened so near Christmas. Edward (7) went from one hype to the next. He was completely unmanageable at school afterwards and they ended up having to keep him in as a punishment every day.*

Who Should Attend Contact Meetings?

The issue of adopters attending contact meetings

There were a number of instances in the study when adopters did not attend
initial contact meetings. This was a crucial issue especially when it occurred
at a stage when the placement was relatively new and the child was
beginning to put down roots. It was rarely the adopter's choice to be
excluded. Frequently adopters were acting on instructions from social
services who worried that the birth family would resent the presence of the
adopters. A quick glance at this type of thinking indicates how easy it was for
the central focus of professional decision making to shift from 'the best
interests of a child' to 'meeting the needs of the birth relatives'.

When adopters were not present some children simply thought that they
had rejected them. This was quite a natural reaction for children who had so
frequently been betrayed by adults. Some had multiple experiences of
disrupted placements. Occasionally adoptive parents were asked to stay in
the vicinity while the social worker supervised the activities of the child and
birth family. Adopters described how children 'fretted', 'kept looking for
them' or 'tried to pull them in to the event'. Even when adopters sixth sense
told them that it was wrong for them to be distanced from this crucial event
many new adopters remained silent, convinced that professionals must know
what is in the child's best interests.

One single adopter who was not allowed to attend the first contact meeting
between Helen (12) and her birth mother could scarcely contain her anger.

> *I was excluded. I wanted to be there. Social services attitude was,*
> *'You're her adoptive mother but for today we'll cut you out'.*

This was the unsatisfactory experience of another highly committed
adoptive family.

> *The proposal for the first contact meeting was put before us as 'fait*
> *accompli'. The meeting was to be at a museum. We were to drop the*
> *boys off and come back four hours later. We disapproved. We were their*
> *new mum and dad. It was only three months into the placement. The*
> *only person involved in the contact meeting that we'd met was the social*
> *worker and we knew that the eldest boy didn't like her. We wanted to be*
> *there all the time. Social services attitude to the birth mother was to treat*
> *her like the Queen Mother and to put her needs first. We were*
> *adamant that if that was what was on offer then we weren't going.*

When considering who should attend contact meetings it is important to
consider the stage of attachment that children may have reached with their
new family. With whom is the primary attachment being constructed? Is this
relationship still at a tenuous stage? Does it need to be promoted? It is vital
that this key parent figure is present at any contact meeting, especially
during the early phases of placement in order to give the child a sense of

security and to convey a non-verbal message to the child about the primary significance of this new relationship. It is also a way of demonstrating to the child that there is a continuity between the past and the present.

Additional People Attending Contact Meetings

When the contact plan was not clearly delineated through a written contact agreement, it was possible for additional people to arrive at contact meetings in an ad hoc manner. Even when contact was formally supervised this could be disconcerting for the child. Stan (10) had annual supervised contact with his birth mother at a social services office. At one meeting he suddenly found himself face-to-face with members of his birth family clamouring for his attention. More than a year had elapsed since he had said Goodbye to them.

Stan's family stood outside the contact centre demanding to get inside to talk with Stan. Stan was awkward. He didn't know what to do. We were on the verge of calling the Police. Granny and uncle had parked their car across the exit so that we couldn't leave. They had been told by social services that they weren't allowed to see him so this was their protest.

Occasionally a foster carer or adopter carried sole responsibility for monitoring the contact relationship. When new faces suddenly appeared at a contact meeting it was hard to make an immediate decision about whether to ban these extra people. Most hesitated to act because they were unsure about how much power they could exert. One foster carer described herself as 'speechless' and 'nonplussed' as she tried to work out how best to protect her vulnerable foster child. Another was dismayed when as many as twelve unfamiliar relatives arrived unexpectedly, especially as each member was demanding the child's undivided attention.

The most worrying situation for the child concerned the sudden appearance at a contact meeting of a birth parent's new partner. Occasionally, this person was able to make a very positive long-term contribution to the child's life. More frequently the exact opposite was the case. The birth mother's series of different partners created the greatest threat. He was often an unstable character who appeared at one meeting and had disappeared from the scene by the time the next contact meeting was due. Another problem arose when birth relatives' new babies arrived without any prior dialogue about whether this was suitable. One adopter described how she constantly feared for the safety of the birth father's new baby because her adopted son had been prescribed medication to quell his aggressive outbursts.

Frequency of Contact Meetings

In some cases there was no definite plan surrounding the frequency of contact meetings between children and their birth relatives. In these situations professionals usually made clear statements about the fact that contact was important but left responsibility for making all the practical arrangements between the adopters and birth relatives. This was far from ideal. It is now a well-documented fact that a 'honeymoon period' can exist at the beginning of an adoption placement when everyone feels euphoric about how well everything is progressing. This study illustrates that 'honeymoon contact' could be a feature of a new placement. In such situations adopters often created a quick rapport with birth relatives. They naively assumed that the relationship would proceed naturally and would not be more complex than any other extended family relationship. Some adopters felt very proud of having been able to achieve such harmony with birth relatives whom they assumed would oppose them. In their enthusiasm they immediately arranged a rapid series of contact meetings. Gradually tensions began to emerge. These could quickly escalate with neither party being sure about how to resolve difficulties because no one had been invested with decision-making power.

In one case where the level of contact recommended by social services between birth relatives and three young children was twice annually, the prospective adopters and birth relatives felt that their relationship was so harmonious that they could increase contact meetings to bi-monthly. Within a short time unexpected tensions began to emerge. After six months this contact that had seemed so promising had spiralled out of control and ended in total failure.

Even when plans for contact were firmly established by professionals, expectations about the frequency of contact that was sustainable by families could be completely unrealistic. When the plan exceeded four times annually, most adoptive families found that this was unmanageable. There were one or two exceptions to this in cases where the birth relatives approved of the adoption placement and were able to establish a positive partnership with the adopters. Mark (6) had contact with his grandmother, uncle and cousin as often as eight times annually. These birth relatives had agreed to sever all connection with Mark's alcoholic birth parents. This arrangement worked well for everyone. Mark loved seeing his birth relatives and each time he returned to his adopters he seemed more confident and more loving. These regular breaks from Mark enabled the adopters to perceive a steady growth in their own attachment to him.

Leon's situation stands in marked contrast to this. He was placed at nine years of age with a single adopter with an expectation that he would retain contact with his birth parents six times annually. After almost three years of regular birth family contact Leon's adopter is adamant that professionals need to listen to her story.

> The level of contact has brought the placement to the brink. It's been so difficult that I haven't felt able to go ahead with the Adoption Order. It hasn't helped Leon to settle. There hasn't been enough time to recover

from one contact before the next one is due. The amount of contact has left him torn and I've been totally exhausted. When I agreed to it I hadn't anticipated how often two months would come round.

Contact at a minimal level of once a year carried its own special difficulties. It became a very poignant event that was well outside the child's norm. Expectations and anxiety levels were high. No one was quite sure how much the birth family might have changed after a year. Children seemed more likely to fantasise about returning to their birth family when contact was maintained at this level.

It was noticeable in fostering placements that professionals often had very high expectations about the level of contact that could be maintained. Examples from the study include fortnightly, three times weekly or monthly contact. Some social workers stated when they were interviewed that degree of contact was often a crucial factor that led them to decide on a fostering rather than an adoption placement. In reality these high levels of contact were often not sustainable. What was expected and what really happened were completely different. Frequently the birth family had rather a chaotic and unpredictable lifestyle that seriously affected their capacity to retain any type of regular arrangement. A contact plan for two sisters, aged ten and five, to see their birth parents every three weeks fell far short of everyone's expectations. When their foster carers reflected on what had actually happened and added up all the birth parent's failed appointments, they calculated that contact that had been planned on a three weekly basis had merely occurred three times during the entire year.

Very occasionally a foster carer was able to work very skilfully with the most challenging birth parent and reach a stage where the number of contact meetings could be increased. Mike was a single foster carer of Ryan (6) and James (4). Their birth father had a criminal record. Social workers were petrified of his aggressive outbursts. When decisions about permanence for the boys were made, the birth father was irate because the court had reduced his contact with the boys from twelve times to twice annually. Gradually the foster father gained the trust of this birth father. After establishing clear boundaries around contact meetings that occurred twice a year, it became feasible to arrange an extra contact meeting. The birth father knew that if he did not act appropriately that contact would again be reduced and social work supervision reintroduced.

The Emotional Impact

It is not surprising to discover that contact with birth parents evoked far higher levels of emotion than contact with other birth relatives. Sometimes the threat posed by a birth parent could be almost unbearable. One adopter explained, 'Your emotions run full blast'.

Another reflected on her turbulent experience:

When I first met James (5) I had an instant bond with him. I felt that he was my son. In an ideal world I would have liked to have given birth to James. Meeting his birth mother was very difficult and stressful. It tore my heart. I was very frightened of meeting this woman. I didn't want to share him with someone who had hurt him. I didn't know how I would deal with him calling her 'mum'.

Keith (5) had only been with his adoptive family for seven months. Professionals had recommended that Keith should have several months to settle in with his new family before contact with his birth father was arranged. His adoptive parents disagreed. They set up the first meeting with his birth father just a few days after he had been placed with them. Keith's adoptive mother soon discovered that handing Keith over to his birth father was one of the hardest experiences of her life.

I've had difficulty emotionally handing Keith over. I can't cope. It guts me. I feel tearful and emotional. I can't cope with him going to his daddy and saying, 'I love you daddy'. I've been devastated. I'm attached.

Most adopters tried to conceal their true emotions from their child.

We do have human feelings of jealousy and dislike. It's OK to feel these things. You have to learn to be cunning and to hold on to these feelings. Try to make yourself distant, which is a difficult thing to do, so that the child can't say, 'My adoptive mum and my real mum didn't get on'.

Childless couples were especially vulnerable. A number of adoptive fathers and mothers described how contact with a birth relative was a constant reminder of the pain of childlessness.

When contact is happening you're openly confronting yourself with the reality that they're not your children. Your human instinct is to close the door and say, 'These are my children'. You want to make it normal. Deep down you have a need to conform to all the other families in the playground.

It was easy for adopters to identify too strongly with a birth parent's sense of loss and to want to gratify the adult. When this happened there was a real danger that the focus of the contact plan could shift from the 'best interests of the child' to meeting the insatiable need of a birth parent.

When you're face-to-face with a birth parent you end up feeling for the parent rather than considering what's best for the kids. Social services get caught up with the birth parents too. The birth father is stating his rights and we're nodding. You become very aware that you're dealing with someone else's emotions. Sometimes it feels like everything is running out of control.

Another adopter felt that she understood a birth parent's loss because of losses in her own life. She ran the risk of prioritising the birth parents rather than the child's needs.

I feel that I can understand a birth parent's agony because of my own sense of loss through being unable to have a second child. My attitude is, 'If I can help the birth parent it's worth trying. Everybody has losses. Why add more losses if I don't have to?'

Some adopters were startled to discover how profoundly affected they were when their child had bad experiences through contact with a birth relative. When their adopted child was rejected by a birth parent they felt the child's pain as deeply as if it was their own. In theory they had envisaged that they would be able to be detached bystanders.

I just didn't anticipate the anger and upset that I would feel on his behalf. The birth parents were so negative. I was frequently moved to tears.

Another adopter spoke about feeling 'bruised inside' when her son's overtures to his birth parents were casually dismissed.

Adopters who had had troubled childhoods were vulnerable. Coming face-to-face with an abusive birth parent was a more poignant experience than reading a child's case file. Some were overwhelmed by painful memories from their own childhood.

Worries About Saying Goodbye

Many adopters spent sleepless nights worrying about what might happen at the end of a contact meeting when it was time to say Goodbye.

My greatest fear was, 'What will I do if they cling to their birth mother and they don't want to come home with us?'

This adopter soon discovered that her fears were unfounded.

. . . as it was they said Goodbye and walked off.

This case was typical of others. Only in one very complex situation did a six-year-old child cling hysterically to her birth father after a contact meeting. This case was exceptional because it was marked by covert sexual activity and emotional blackmail between the birth father and the child. In all other situations the actual moment of saying Goodbye was largely uneventful.

Summary of Key Points

- **The timing of first contact meetings**

  When birth relatives approve of an adoption placement, a contact meeting can be a very positive and reassuring experience for the child when it occurs during the early weeks and months of the placement.

  When birth relatives disapprove of an adoption placement, it is advisable to delay the first contact meeting for several months to enable the child to establish relationships in the adoptive family without the distraction of torn loyalties.

  When contact with birth relatives is radically altered or terminated at the point of transferring to a plan for permanency for the child, it is vital that time is invested with the child, explaining the reasons for this change. Otherwise this issue is liable to overshadow the child's ability to settle in placement.

- **Contact on special days**

  Birthdays and Christmas are emotive times. The giving and receiving of gifts can be a very sensitive issue for children and their birth relatives. Arranging contact meetings at these sensitive times may add to the complexity of contact relationships.

- **Who should attend?**

  It is important to have a written contact agreement that specifies who should attend contact meetings in order to minimise risk to the child.

  When a contact meeting is arranged during the early phases of an adoption placement it is important that an adoptive parent be present at the meeting to provide the children with a sense of security and a clear message about the primary and permanent significance of this new parental relationship.

- **Frequency of contact**

  It is unlikely that a level of contact between children and their adult birth relatives that extends beyond four times annually will be manageable or practically viable in an adoption placement. Expectations that premanent foster carers could sustain levels of contact set as high as fortnightly or monthly were often totally unrealistic.

- **The need for an intermediary**

  It is unwise to leave the practicalities of initial contact planning solely in the hands of adopters and birth relatives with no intermediary. With such a complex relationship tensions are liable to occur that are best resolved through the intervention of a third party.

- **The emotional impact**

  Torn emotions are liable to affect everyone involved in a contact relationship. Childless couples are vulnerable. Contact with birth parents is likely to trigger pain associated with childlessness. Adopters and foster carers who have had an abusive childhood may have to face the pain of their own childhood as they come face-to-face with abusive birth relatives.

- **Children saying Goodbye to birth relatives**

  Adopters' concerns about children being unable to extricate themselves from birth parents at the conclusion of contact meetings were not realised. Usually children were happy to return to their adoptive home without any major problems.

CHAPTER 5

The Joys, Difficulties, and Aftermath of Contact

This chapter examines the joys and difficulties associated with contact with adult birth relatives such as birth parents, grandparents, aunts and uncles. Chapter 6 focuses on issues arising in sibling contact.

Sixty-eight children had had some contact with at least one adult birth relative since placement. Twelve children had started and then lost contact with at least one adult birth relative. In a few instances social services had terminated the relationship due to concerns about the adverse effects on a child's welfare. In other situations a birth relative had gradually lost interest or the relationship between the adoptive and the birth family had broken down irretrievably.

The Joys of Contact

Relationships between children and their birth relatives were highly emotive especially as these relatives had frequently been either directly or indirectly involved in the abuse of children. Of course there were positive aspects but there were usually negative features also. It was the complex interweaving of positive and negative features that made the retention of these relationships so challenging for everyone involved. The sentiments expressed by Karl (9) to his adopters about his birth mother Cheryl immediately after a terrifying temper tantrum typify the ebbing and flowing of feelings that so frequently underpinned the reality of contact.

I want to love Cheryl but I want to hate her as well.
I want to love her because I didn't want to get taken away.
I want to love Cheryl because she was my real mum.
I want to remember that Cheryl loved me a bit.
I want to hate Cheryl because she didn't feed me properly.
She didn't pay attention to me.
I want to hate her more than I love her.

Many children had a real need to retain contact with their birth relatives. This was not so much because of a strong emotional bond but rather because they wanted to ensure that their birth relatives were safe and well. Children worried about birth parents who were addicted to alcohol or drugs, the parent who was a known prostitute, the inept parent or the parent with health problems. Several children worried that their birth parents might die. Face-to-face contact quelled these anxieties and enabled the child to get on with day-to-day living.

Lucy (14) has not been able to retain contact with her birth mother because to do so would place her at risk. However, through contact with her maternal grandmother she has been able to achieve a degree of psychological closeness to her birth mother.

Lucy needs to have a link back to her mother. She's not particularly close to her grandmother. She uses grandmother as a source of information about her birth mother and sister.

After these contact meetings Lucy is moody, sullen and provocative as she works through painful feelings associated with a neglected childhood.

Danny (11) has had contact with his maternal grandmother. His adopters feel that seeing his grandmother has enabled him to work through his grief for the loss of other members of his birth family.

Seeing granny helped him to let go. She provided a consistent thread that ran through his life. He wanted to hold and cuddle her and make sure that she was alive. He used to get upset and angry when they parted. It brought up all the losses.

The answers to down-to-earth questions that left children curious and perplexed were rarely recorded in case files. Face-to-face contact opened up opportunities for children to pose sensitive questions:

Did mummy cry when the policeman came?

When daddy kicked you, did it hurt?

This notion of children's need to recycle their grief and pain is helpfully described by Claudia Jewett (1984):

Children in particular often need to revisit and re-address grief experiences and their feelings about them as they grow and develop and sometimes their behaviour or recurring concerns will signal that they need help.

Some children were struggling with identity issues. They wanted to understand from whom they had inherited certain physical characteristics or special talents.

These are the kind of questions that Sean (11) wanted answered. Why he's got big hands? Why he's tall? Why he's good at music? Why his birth parents behaved the way they did?

Occasionally there was a moment of realisation for the child when the stark reality of why a birth parent could not provide adequate care seemed to dawn. After her second contact with her birth mother Marian (7) cried.

Mummy Dawn is hopeless. She can't look after herself and she can't look after me. My mum's sad.

Although these were traumatic moments for children, some adopters felt heartened that their child was able to face reality and to make comparisons between their birth and adoptive family. After meeting her birth mother Sonia (11) hugged her adoptive mother and said:

You're a big strong mummy that can keep me safe.

It was easy for the children's anger to be projected inappropriately on to their adopter or foster carer. Face-to-face contact enabled some children to direct their anger towards an abusive parent. There were instances of children losing control during contact meetings and actually hitting a birth parent. In one exceptional case an 11-year-old boy went to a contact meeting with his Life Story Book and challenged his birth father to take him through his abusive life history. The fact that his birth father had physically abused him throughout his childhood made this meeting especially poignant. Liam (10) also tried to get his birth mother to openly acknowledge responsibility for her actions.

> *At the last contact Liam looked and looked at his birth mother in a deep way. Before that he'd been polite but he never wanted much to do with her. He'd answer her quickly. If she touched him he'd try to get away as soon as possible. At the last contact he asked her, 'Why was I covered in bruises?' She said, 'You weren't'. He said, 'Yes I was'.*

There were moments of healing for children who had been abused when a birth relative was simply able to utter the word 'Sorry'. Sean (11) found it helpful that his birth mother had almost apologised for failing to protect him from violence. Following this dialogue with her he has said to his adoptive mother:

> *I think I can understand a bit better what my 'first mum' has been through.*

Children benefited from witnessing firsthand that a positive relationship existed between their adoptive parents or foster carers and their birth parents. Phil (13), Richard (12) and Jason (10) looked cautiously to their adoptive parents, hoping that they would endorse their positive sentiments.

> *They would say to us, 'It was great to see them. Weren't they nice?' They wanted us to confirm that.*

Minor positive interactions between adopters and birth parents became highly significant to the child. Robin (9) was impressed as he watched his adoptive father purchase a can of Coca-Cola for his birth mother. Shane (9) smiled as he said to his adoptive mother:

> *You're really good with mummy Kathryn. You're really nice to her.*

The positive impact of a birth parent being able to tell a child directly that they approved of their adoptive parents was enormous. One adopter described it 'as the best gift in the whole world'.

The Difficulties Associated with Contact

Use of mobile telephones

Mobile telephones were a powerful weapon that some children used to make secret conversations with their birth relatives. There were incidents of birth relatives passing their mobile telephone numbers surreptitiously to children and teenagers during contact meetings. One teenager made daily mobile calls to his birth family over several months. This was only discovered when the adoptive family received an astronomical telephone account. By this time the teenager and his birth family had worked out a sophisticated plot to enable him to abscond from his adoptive family.

Child Protection Issues

Risk of encountering an abuser

Face-to-face contact opened up the risk of a child meeting a previous abuser. When there was no written contact agreement, it was relatively easy for anyone to appear at a contact meeting. The turbulence of the birth family meant that birth mothers often had transient romantic relationships with high risk males. Some partners had served prison sentences. Jenny (8) and Roseanne (7) were always tense when they went to meet their birth mother. On one occasion the birth mother's new boyfriend appeared with a camcorder. Although he had never met the children before he lifted them on to his knee and began to cuddle them. Jenny and Roseanne's foster carers had repeatedly encouraged them never to sit on a stranger's knee.

When a contact relationship between a child and a grandparent was going well it was easy for the grandparents to promise never to disclose the child's new name or address to any relative who had maltreated the child. When the contact relationship had broken down there were risks that these promises would be broken. There was one instance of a disgruntled grandmother revealing confidential information to the children's birth mother who had a serious criminal record. The adopters wondered what they would do if this aggressive birth mother decided to appear at their address.

Anita (12) always enjoyed her sister Jane's visits. Jane lived with her birth mother. After one visit Anita's adopters decided to drive Jane back to the birth family's house and that they would all stop for a brief visit. That was not an unusual occurrence. However, the events that followed were unforgettable as Anita found herself face-to-face with one of her birth mother's previous partners. Anita grew agitated. She whispered his name to her adoptive mother. Anita had vivid memories of this man's physical threats to her and her birth mother. She had almost managed to force these incidents to the back of her mind. Suddenly it felt as if everything in her past had become a cruel reality again.

Geographical closeness between the adoptive family and the birth family created a degree of risk too. Phil's adopter lived just twelve miles from his birth family. Although Phil was 15 years old he was emotionally immature and exceptionally vulnerable. One day when he was walking along the street he met his birth brother. He dared to ask him to take him to his birth mother's house. Phil stood on the doorstep with very mixed emotions. He was proud of his achievement but far too terrified to press the doorbell. This incident had a profound impact on the stability of his placement as Phil began to run away and to sleep rough. His adopter admitted that she felt uncomfortable about what had happened and 'totally out of control' of Phil's birth family connections.

Marian (9) took her adopter to a house within easy walking distance and said:

> *That's granny's house. You thought that I didn't know.*

Then, as if she was too frightened to acknowledge the painful memories that she had about this cruel grandmother she quickly added:

> *My grandma's London is a different London to your London.*

Sexual innuendo

Professionals were suspicious that Carole (5) and Tracey (3) had suffered sexual abuse. Allegations against an older brother had not been proven. Their birth mother was a prostitute and there was no doubt that the girls had witnessed inappropriate sexual activity. Both girls were having regular contact with their birth father under the supervision of their foster mother. The degree of covert sexual activity between Carole and her father was very worrying.

> *Carole wanted to be with her birth father. She'd try to get him to leave the room and take her to the toilet. It was sexual. She would put her hand in his pocket and touch his crotch. He was nervous of physical contact with the girls and always looking for my response. She would whisper little secrets to him, telling him that she wanted to live with him. At the same time she was telling the social worker that she didn't want to live with him. I watched him manipulate her. I watched him cling to her and work her up until she cried.*

> *The power that he had over Carole was unbelievable. He was a child himself and very controlling. He played one child off against another. He'd bring a gift for one and not for the other. He'd whisper to her about the gifts that he had brought her. Carole had a close but very strange relationship with him. Physical contact between them was not appropriate. Carole used female wiles and sexual games. She was having a powerful sexual relationship with him. He gave me the creeps.*

The lure of the birth family's criminal lifestyle

When Peter (8) was placed with his adopter the Judge recommended that all contact with his birth family should be terminated. The Guardian ad Litem had recommended contact twice a year but the Judge refused to endorse this. However, Peter did not want to break his family links. His adopter agreed to endorse his wish for contact and he has supervised all contact visits. At 16 years old Peter has suddenly wanted to see more and more of his birth family. His adoptive father is clear about what motivates him.

During the past two months he's wanted more and more contact. His big brother is into car crime so it's very exciting for him. The birth family live far too near us. That's a disadvantage.

Another serious problem was that birth parents with a history of addiction tried to pass alcohol and drugs to children and teenagers during contact meetings.

Further emotional abuse

Although it was not feasible to interview birth relatives for this study it was frequently apparent that they needed far more preparation and support if they were going to be able to use contact meetings in a way that was in the best interests of the child. Some birth relative's attitudes and behaviour placed children under so much pressure during contact meetings that what was happening could be considered to be a form of emotional abuse.

Initially Leon (9) was very enthusiastic about seeing his birth parents. He told his social worker:

I want to see them a lot.

However, the reality was very difficult to tolerate as his birth parents were so rejecting of him. They were very immature and their own childlike needs seemed to predominate.

Leon was less keen on contact when he discovered that his birth mother was not supportive of his relationship with me. She would have a 'go' at him. 'Where's my Mother's Day card?' We'd take photos to the meetings but his birth mother wouldn't look at them. He always took presents for them. They never brought him anything.

When we were on holiday he bought a picture frame and put a photo of himself in it. He gave it to his birth mother. She took a quick look and said, 'What do I need that for?' She threw it away. He was devastated. She moaned to him, 'I've never had a holiday'.

Danny was five when he joined his adoptive family. He loved seeing his grandmother. However, she lived with Danny's birth parents and they always interrogated her about Danny's progress when she returned home. Danny found her questions unnerving.

He'd put his arms round her and she would push him away. She'd say, 'Show me your teeth'. She'd demand to have him measured and weighed. She'd put pressure on him to succeed in school. She'd test his spelling. She had no concept of his emotional needs. Monitoring his physical needs was the only way that the birth family could feel that they were exerting some control.

Names and Surnames

Children who were placed for adoption often chose to change their surname as soon as they joined their new family. Many enrolled at school under their new name. This was a highly controversial issue at contact meetings especially for birth parents. Some birth parents caused consternation by trying to persuade children to revert back to their original name. Other birth relatives took advantage of any private moment with the child to extort their new surname and address.

The terms Mum and Dad were even more contentious. Prior to her first contact meeting with her birth mother Natasha (9) asked her adoptive mother, 'Will I call her mummy?' When she was told that she could she looked quizzical and responded:

. . . but I call you Mummy. I feel torn in half.

Some birth grand-parents exploded during contact meetings because children refused to refer to their original parents as Mum and Dad. Some contact arrangements with grandparents had to be terminated because they were rigidly promoting birth parents rights on this matter and unsettling the equilibrium of placements.

Letters from birth parents often contained the child's original surname and were signed Mummy and Daddy. Sean (11) was angry when he received a letter that began 'to our beloved son'. He retorted, 'I'm not their son. They don't want me'. Andrew (10) reacted angrily when his adopter began reading a loving letter to him from his birth mother. By the time she had finished the first sentence he had fled from the room. She left the letter lying on the kitchen table thinking that he might like to peruse it in his own time. When Andrew found it his face turned red with anger and he ripped up the correspondence into tiny shreds.

How could these difficulties have been overcome? Careful preparation surrounding the issue of names is obviously essential for all parties before embarking on face-to-face contact. It was clear from many examples cited that adult birth relatives had often not had preparation for contact and were consequently unaware of the potential impact of their words and actions on the child. The following methods of preparation are recommended:

- Careful preparatory discussion with all parties involved in contact.
- Life Story work with the child providing an opportunity for the child to think about names to be used for birth relatives and for foster carers and adopters. This preparatory work can then clarify for the child exactly what names can be utilised during contact meetings.
- Written contact agreements that clarify names to be used.

Distorted Roles and Relationships

Many of the children in this study derived from families that were deeply disturbed. Parental and children's roles were often quite distorted. Some of these disturbed patterns became evident in contact relationships.

When living with their birth family children had often been forced to take on an inappropriate parental role in order to keep the family safe. This was the only way in which survival was possible in such a dangerous family environment. Valmai (7) remembers when she was four years old how she used to teach her mother to cook and how she had dialled 999 when there was a family emergency. When Natasha was four she had to do all the family shopping and call the family doctor when her mother's depression became life threatening. When Richard (9) was placed with his new family they described him in the following way:

Richard was the eldest in the family. The others had looked to him as a lifeline. He was the father figure. When he came to us he was nine: but he was like a teenager, a dad and a nine-year-old. After he came here he shed years, like shedding onion layers. He became younger and younger and gradually he went back to younger than he was. Then he went to his normal age.

When contact with a birth parent occurred children often reverted to previous modes of behaviour by taking on the nurturing parental role while birth parents often treated children as equals, confiding in them about adult concerns, serious health problems and sexual exploits. Adopters and foster carers who had invested time helping children regain their childhood often found that contact with birth parents could set back months of progress.

Poor Quality Interaction Between Children and Their Birth Relatives

The quality of interaction between birth parents and their children was generally very poor. One adopter described it as 'wooden contact'. Most birth parents had no idea how to play or communicate with their child. Sometimes it was apparent that the birth parent's view of the child's stage of development had become 'frozen in time' at the point the parent had been forced to relinquish the child. Gifts that parents produced often reflected this. One birth mother used to unwrap a baby toy or a dummy for her 10-year-old daughter.

When a birth parent made false promises, children's hopes were raised, and quickly dashed. Telling children that preparations were underway for their return home had major implications for children who were easily unsettled in their permanent placements. Children were frequently promised expensive gifts that failed to materialise. Brian (16) had made up his mind that he never wanted to see his birth father again unless he produced the mobile telephone that he had promised.

There were countless examples in the study, of a birth parent feigning illness. The most common scenario was for the birth mother to state that she was dying of cancer. Such statements were disconcerting for children and usually a deliberate attempt by a birth parent to become the focus of attention.

Favouring one child and rejecting another was an extreme difficulty. This was not only a problem for the rejected child but often the favoured child felt uncomfortable too. Lucy (14) always got £20 for Christmas from her birth grandparents while her younger brother Lee (9) got £5. Stephen (7) and Natalie (6) are siblings who had contact with their birth father every six months. Contact was an exceptionally positive experience for Stephen but an outright rejection for Natalie.

> *The birth father has this big thing about having a son. He never lived with Natalie. He really only wants to see Stephen. Stephen benefits but Natalie is excluded. Natalie stops eating the week before dad comes. She is very negative and she becomes quite aggressive afterwards. She picks up the undercurrents but if I was to say, 'You can come and see Stephen only', Natalie would go berserk with jealousy.*

Physical contact between children and birth relatives

Physical contact between children and birth relatives often left everyone feeling uncomfortable. Some children felt awkward and distressed by birth relatives demands for physical affection. At other times children were rebuffed by a birth parent who simply did not know how to respond.

> *I said to Victor (12) 'Do you want to give mum a hug?' He went up to her and she said, 'What do you want?' He just stood and looked and then came back to me. That hurt me more than anything but you can't say what you think.*

Special Occasions in the Birth Family

Weddings

A number of adoptive families were invited to a birth parent's wedding. One adoptive father lay awake examining the pros and cons of attending the birth mother's wedding with his two boys. Having summoned the courage to broach the topic with his boys he was surprised to discover how unemotional they were about what was happening.

> *I said to Robin (13), 'Your mum's getting married'. 'Phew', he said. 'Throw the invitation in the fire.'*
>
> *Then I told Victor (12). 'Will it be in a big hotel?' he asked. 'If not, I'm not going.'*

A number of girls in the study were bridesmaids or flower girls at a birth parent's wedding. Some adopters proudly displayed photographs in their living room of these special occasions.

A birth family get-together

Sharon (12) really wanted to attend a special birth family celebration. She had only been living with her adoptive family for seven months. Her adopters were invited too.

Her adopters still remember the stress of the situation as both families wanted to claim Sharon as their own. Decisions about who should sit next to whom and who should travel with whom had not been discussed with Sharon in advance. She found it impossible to know what to do as she found her loyalties pulled in different directions. Sharon's adoptive father was surprised at the strength of his reaction.

Grandma had a house warming meal. We found it stressful. Sharon sat with us at the meal. The birth mother kept taking her out and having secret conversations with her. They were like two giggly schoolgirls. Then she decided to go with the birth family in their car. My blood pressure was high and I was livid. The birth mother is completely insensitive to the fact that her daughter is adopted. The birth mother isn't our sort of person. She's the type of person we'd usually avoid. She's over the top.

After that I shouted at everyone, including Sharon and the social workers.

Death and dying

One implication of face-to-face contact was that some children had to cope with the pain associated with the death of a birth relative. Debra (18) still feels angry because social workers took so long to organise contact with her birth mother. Debra was 15 years old when she asked her social worker to make the necessary contact arrangements. Months of delay ensued. Suddenly the birth mother became critically ill and was dying in hospital. Meeting her and other relatives in intensive care was an unforgettable experience.

When we went to intensive care all the relatives were there. They were wild. There was a punch up. It was a shambles. We were surrounded by grieving relatives.

Leon was 12 years old when his birth mother died suddenly of a massive cerebral haemorrhage. He had been having regular contact with her. Just prior to her death he had been going through a stage of being very angry and dismissive of her. Now his adopter had to face the daunting task of helping him cope with a torrent of ambivalent feelings.

At first Leon was shocked. His initial reaction was, 'Well that's contact out of the way. That's good'. He asked me, 'What did you do when you heard?' I said, 'I cried'. Then he cried. He wanted to see her body so we went to the hospital mortuary. His birth father phoned. He was drunk. We wrote a prayer. Leon's birth sister said she'd pick a hymn. Leon decided that he didn't want to get involved in choosing anything. He said that he didn't like her. She was a horrible mother but he still loved her. The funeral presented a very positive picture. Leon said, 'The vicar lied'. He was frightened of meeting other relatives. When we got to the church there was no space. The family were boozed. We ended up in the front seat facing all the people. A man came up to him and said, 'Are you Leon? I'm your uncle'.

After the funeral we had planned the afternoon. We were going to play monopoly. I asked Leon if he wanted to go back and look at the flowers. He said, 'No. It's finished'.

Danny was ten years old when his grandmother died. When he joined his adoptive family it was planned that he would see her every month but this proved to be an unrealistic plan and contact was reduced to four times a year. As her health declined contact was reduced still further. Grandmother's death affected Danny deeply. His behaviour deteriorated at school and he was excluded for a time. His adopters arranged for him to have professional counselling on a weekly basis for one school term. At the point of transferring to secondary school Danny seemed to develop a new zest for life and he made the decision that he could manage without counselling. With a new confidence he told his adoptive mother:

I think I can think about my nan in my own time now. If I need to talk about it I will.

The Aftermath of Contact

Siblings' differing attitudes to contact

Siblings often had an unequal commitment to contact. It was common for one to yearn for it and exhibit a major reaction after it had happened, while the other just drifted along in an indifferent manner with no obvious investment in the process and no apparent after effects. The child who wanted contact was always the one who had developed a significant relationship with the birth relative prior to entry into the care system. However, this was also a very vulnerable child who had frequently undertaken a parenting role while living with the birth family. This child usually exhibited a high level of turbulence after a contact meeting. Natasha is now ten years old and her younger sister Paula is six. Natasha lived with her birth mother until she was four while Paula was admitted to foster care at birth and consequently never had a chance to form a close bond with her mother.

The trauma of the first contact with the birth mother was great for Natasha. She was high. There's strong feelings there. She found it very hard. It brought her close to the edge. There was just nothing from Paula.

Positive aftermath

Eight children reacted very positively to contact meetings. Seeing their birth relatives released them from constant worry about them. Keith (5) a hyper-active child described contact as 'wanting to see his daddy's eyes'. He always seemed calmer after he had spent time with him. Brendan (15) displayed deeply disturbing behaviour with ritualistic patterns.

> *Brendan continues here as if he were a lodger. It's impossible to get him into the family group. He spends all his time in his room with the curtains drawn, watching TV. He has no friends and he's always angry.*

His foster carers observed that after contact with his birth father he seemed to be 'more normal' and 'freed up a bit'.

Frozen emotions

Three children reacted to contact by switching off any emotional response. Despite the fact that Tricia (12) suffered emotional, physical and sexual abuse she exhibits no real reaction after meeting her birth relatives. This is her foster carer's observation about how Tricia copes:

> *Contact has a place in Tricia's life but she doesn't carry baggage out of it. Contact is a compartment. It doesn't affect other areas of her life. She shows no obvious signs of upset. She just lets it happen.*

Fahad was 14 years old when his older adopted brother died. Fahad had great difficulty expressing any emotion but at the funeral he began to weep uncontrollably. As his adopters watched him they felt that the tears he shed that day were years of repressed feelings for himself as well as genuine grief for his adopted brother.

When William (12) was told that his birth mother had refused to have any further contact with him because of his sexualised behaviour he simply retreated to his bedroom and closed down all conversation about her. No one could coax him to speak about how he felt. He just 'cut her out as if she was dead'.

More extreme reactions

Some children had an extreme reaction following their first contact meeting. However, as contact became a regular feature difficulties subsided and they learned to cope. Sharon is now 17 years old and has been with her adoptive family for five years. Initially contact with her birth family was very stressful and would result in visible scarring to her body through self-mutilation. Five years later she is able to 'take it in her stride'.

One or two adopters felt that they should have delayed the first contact meeting to give the child longer to settle. Scott was eight when he joined his adoptive family. His first year was marked by impulsive and destructive behaviour and he was very rejecting of his adoptive mother who described Scott's placement as 'hanging by a thread'. When he met his birth mother about four months into placement, Scott's difficult behaviour became totally unmanageable and the placement almost disrupted.

He was loyal to his birth mother. After seeing her he was so distraught in the middle of the night. I expected that he might be wobbly but not for it to be so extreme. He was very angry with me for hours after contact. It took him several weeks to relax again. There was evidence of setback. He went on and on about violent scenes from videos. He went on and on about blood and about violence in an obsessive way. I think contact should have been delayed for a year and then stepped up gradually. As soon as the year was up things were being repeated and he relaxed a lot. He'd been a year in the same place and seen the same things happen again.

One problem for Leon (9) was that he was having contact with his birth relatives every two months. He had insufficient time to recover from the trauma of one contact before the next one was due. Besides he was experiencing rejection from his birth mother practically every time he saw her. He was also picking up strong vibes that she did not approve of his adoptive family and the atmosphere between his adoptive mother and the birth mother was exceptionally tense. It is not surprising that a close friend of his adoptive mother described him as 'a little boy drowning'.

He would be tearful and have nightmares. He'd ask me to come and bath him and he'd need a hot water bottle. He'd want me to fluff up his pillow. He'd become extremely clingy and babyish and demanding of physical contact. He'd be hostile and aggressive and unable to co-ordinate his limbs. He'd fall over. He'd be unable to listen or to follow simple instructions. He was soiling and smearing. He was totally disorganised. He'd switch in two minutes.

Carole (5), a foster child, was acting out a powerful sexual relationship with her birth father during contact. The aftermath of contact was overwhelming.

Breaking Carole's routine made her quite hysterical. She'd make strange grovelling noises. She'd kick and spit and punch and be sexually provocative. She'd cry and it was extremely difficult to get her calm.

When Andrew (10) said that he did not want to see his birth mother everyone assumed that he was playing psychological games. When stress built up inside him he acted out sexually. When he sexually abused another child in his adoptive family his placement disrupted. His psychiatric assessment stated that contact with his birth mother had not been in Andrew's best interests.

Ryan is now 12 years old. Despite the fact that he has been seeing his birth father regularly during his six year foster placement, he still holds torrents of anger inside that can burst out into the open at any time.

Ryan was playing basketball and trying to attract his birth father's attention. He was shouting, sulking and locking himself in the loo. At 7 p.m. that evening he blew: screaming, shouting and swearing for hours. There were vibes beforehand. It was a bit like watching a volcano.

It's frightening for him to be so enraged. The tension inside him is incredible. You just can't leave the power in there.

Length of the aftermath

Some children recovered from the aftermath of contact within a few days. Others took weeks and even months to work through their feelings. One adoptive mother of an 11-year-old boy had twenty years experience of working with children within a residential establishment. She had watched many children work through the traumatic feelings associated with contact. She had anticipated that her adopted son would recover within days of contact. Instead she was startled to discover that it actually took him about six weeks.

Sometimes it was the school that had to handle the worst aspects of children's behaviour. Some adopters felt that it was advisable to inform the school when contact was happening so that they could respond sensitively to the child's vulnerability. Others were highly critical of the attitude of school staff. One teacher put forward a proposal to exclude Natalie (6) for three weeks following each contact meeting because her aggressive outbursts were disrupting the entire class.

Factors affecting aftermath

Children's difficulties following contact were exacerbated when:
- Adopters or foster carers and birth relatives were unable to establish a positive relationship.
- The birth relative's disapproval of the placement was apparent to the child.
- The birth relative was unable to accept the child's new name and status.
- The birth relative exhibited rejection of the child during contact meetings.
- The frequency of contact meetings did not provide sufficient recovery time for the child. In adoption placements, this was usually when contact meetings exceeded four times annually.
- Contact was instigated at too early a stage in the placement. This was a particular factor when birth relatives disapproved of the placement and children's loyalties were therefore likely to be torn in different directions at a stage when they were still emotionally insecure in their new placement.

The aftermath for other adopted or foster children

Children's contact experiences inevitably impinged on other foster and adopted children in the family. Debra (18) and Brendan (15) are not blood relatives but they have been placed in the same family. Debra is an extrovert who has put a lot of energy into retaining contact with five birth relatives.

Although her birth family have enormous problems Debra boasts about them. Brendan has a different personality. He lacks confidence and isolates himself from everyone. His birth mother has declined to see him; his younger sister has experienced one disrupted placement after another and has shown little interest in Brendan. His birth father raises his hopes by making promises that he fails to fulfil and has been very half hearted about seeing him. Instead of criticising his own birth family Brendan projects all his anger on to Debra's family. He calls her mother a prostitute. This is in fact an accurate description of his own birth mother who has let him down so badly.

Sean (11) and Barry (9) are both adopted. They have no blood relationship. Sean sees his birth parents and siblings on a regular basis but Barry's birth family have declined to see him. Sean has explained to Barry 'You're not really missing anything'.

Sean's situation intensifies Barry's feelings of rejection. When Sean was being interviewed Barry was eager to share his viewpoint.

> When Sean gets to see his mum and dad it makes me feel angry: miserable angry that I don't get my turn of seeing my real parents. I try to keep my feelings inside myself.

Cherie (8) is one of three adopted children. The other two are brothers who have regular birth family contact. Cherie has been told by social services that contact is not in her best interests.

> Cherie is angry with social services. She says, 'It's a pity that I couldn't see the social worker and give her a punch in the eye'. The feelings are there anyway. Her anger is ongoing but the boys' contact highlights it for her. She talks about it when she's in the bath when she's reflective and open and when we're both static.

There was only one sibling group in the study where one child had contact with his birth parents and the others did not. This was a very complex case. Originally there were no plans for contact for Robert (13), Ashley (12), Russell (8) and Jo (9). Robert had been the father figure while living in the birth family. He had the clearest memories of the distressing experiences that they had all been subjected to in their birth family. Robert's need to see his birth parents was overwhelming and at times dominated the placement. He made it difficult for the other siblings to settle by constantly referring to the past. The others had little conscious awareness of the shocking childhood experiences that preyed on his mind. After three years in placement Robert's wish to see his birth parents was granted. Within a few weeks his unsettled adoption placement had disrupted.

> Robert was feeding a lot of poison about the birth parents to the other children. He kept goading the others. He had been the father figure that had lashed out punishment. He tried to keep that up. He had a battle with loyalties. He couldn't come to terms with his emotions. All his feelings were passed on to the others.

The Overall Impact on Children of Contact with Adult Birth Relatives

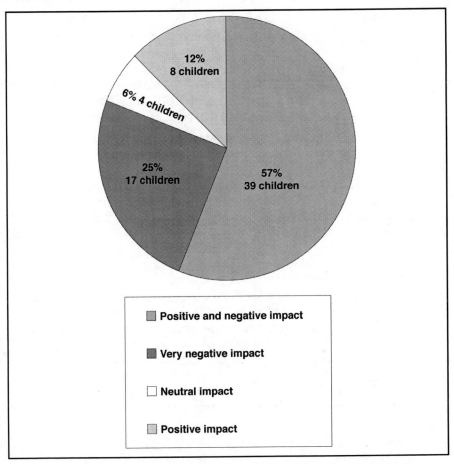

Figure 12: Impact of contact with adult birth relatives on children

Figure 12 depicts how contact with adult birth relatives affected children. The information presented is based on the views of adopters, foster carers, social workers and children themselves.

Positive contact

Eight children (12 per cent) found contact to be a very positive experience. All the children in this group were wholehearted in their enthusiasm to see their birth relatives. Adopters and foster carers believed that contact was beneficial for children. Birth relatives and adopters or foster carers were able to form a trusting and respectful relationship where each family 'adopted' the other. Children took contact in their stride and there were no real indications of contact triggering negative feelings or producing troubled behaviour.

Neutral contact

Four children (6 per cent) appeared to be quite indifferent to contact. In these cases the child had never established a relationship with the birth relative that was significant. There had never been an opportunity for a close bond to take place. Often children in this group were part of a sibling group and a brother or sister really wanted contact. One sibling could be zealous about contact while another showed all the signs of indifference and appeared unaffected by contact meetings.

Positive and negative contact

Thirty-nine children (57 per cent) who fitted into this group represented the majority. Most wanted to see their birth relatives but the reality was full of emotion and at times quite overwhelming. The sentiments of one 12 year old boy expressed after he heard his birth mother had died typify the ebbing and flowing of emotions that made contact so difficult for everyone.

> *I didn't like my birth mother. She was a horrible mother: but I think I still loved her.*

If his feelings had fitted neatly into one category of either loving her or detesting her, seeing her would have been more straightforward.

Throughout childhood birth relatives had often proved to be unreliable, immature and irresponsible. Some of these negative characteristics re-emerged during contact meetings. Painful and angry emotions were aroused. Adopters and foster carers tried to build positive relationships with birth relatives but they often found themselves struggling in a sea of negative emotions that they knew they had to try to conceal from the child. Children's sense of loyalty to their new family was sometimes undermined by the birth family, leaving the child 'torn in two'. There were happy moments but also moments of sad realisation when the birth family's inadequacy left everyone devastated.

Very negative contact

Seventeen children (25 per cent) fitted into this category. Within this group children were often rejected during contact or discarded as less worthwhile than a sibling. Due to some birth relatives limited awareness of a child's emotional needs it was possible for a child to be exposed to further emotional harm during contact meetings.

Of the 68 children who had contact with an adult birth relative, ten placements disrupted. The reasons for disruption were multifarious and complex. However, in six cases that appear in this group, either social workers, foster carers or adopters stated that contact was considered to be the key factor that caused disruption to occur. In each of these six cases contact was with one or both birth parents. In a further two cases within this group adopters stated that the difficulties associated with contact were so great that it brought 'the placement to the brink of disruption'.

Summary of Key Points

Overall theme

Positive aspects of contact were usually complexly interlinked with negative aspects.

Positive features of contact between children and adult birth relatives

- Children were reassured about the welfare of their birth relatives and consequently able to get on with life without distraction.
- Adopters and foster carers gained additional background information and new insights into the birth family's ethos. This facilitated giving the child explanations about their childhood.
- Prior to and after contact meetings some children were able to have very open and natural conversations with their adopters and foster carers about some of the difficult experiences that had occurred while they were living in their birth family.
- Children were able to get direct answers from their birth relatives about gaps in their understanding of their family life.
- Children were able to explore identity issues by discovering which birth relatives they resembled or from whom they had acquired special talents.
- It was reassuring for the child when birth relatives were able to express approval of their new family and for their placement.
- Children found it helpful when they could see tangible evidence of their adoptive parent accepting a birth relative, e.g. adoptive parent buying a drink for a birth parent; adoptive parent speaking in a sensitive and kind manner to the birth parent; adoptive family and birth family able to join together harmoniously in a social event.
- A degree of emotional healing for the child was feasible when a birth relative was able to apologise directly to the child about abusive episodes that had occurred during childhood.

Risk factors

The risk of a child encountering an abusive birth relative was increased when:

- There was no written contact agreement specifying who should attend contact meetings.
- The longer-term risks associated with using the adopter's home as the contact venue had not been fully assessed.

- The adoptive family resided in a geographical location close to the birth family.

Face-to-face contact opened opportunities for a child to be attracted to and become involved directly in the birth family's life of crime.

In some instances the more widespread use of mobile telephones facilitated unplanned contact with birth relatives with its inherent dangers.

Negative aspects

- The quality of a contact relationship between a child and a birth relative could be covertly abusive and rejecting of the child.
- Distorted roles and relationships between adults and children that were frequently a feature of dysfunctional family life were liable to be re-enacted during contact meetings and to set back the progress of the placement.
- The child who had assumed a parenting role for other family members while living in the birth family was exceptionally vulnerable. This child's need for contact was likely to be intense. The birth relative and child's role often became reversed during contact meetings and this child was liable to experience the greatest negative aftermath.
- A birth family's inability to accept a child's new name and surname could be deeply traumatic for a child arousing feelings of divided loyalties and destabilising the placement. This issue needs to be addressed by adopters, the child, and birth relatives prior to the commencement of contact.
- Contact planned at too early a stage of placement especially when the birth relative is opposed to the placement plan, too frequent contact meetings, and a negative relationship between the adopters or foster carers and the birth relatives, are all factors that exacerbate the child's level of distress following contact, and are liable to de-stabilise the placement.

Summary of difficult behaviours and feelings exhibited by children following contact

- absconding
- aggression towards children and adults
- concentration loss
- inability to follow simple instructions
- eneuresis and encopresis
- smearing faeces
- deterioration in schoolwork
- defiant controlling behaviour
- disorganised behaviour
- distress
- eating problems
- mute reaction
- projection of anger on to different members of the adoptive or foster family
- regression to infantile stage of development
- self mutilation
- sexualised behaviour
- switching off emotionally
- uncontrollable outbursts of anger
- poor co-ordination of limbs
- withdrawal
- fear of being removed by birth relative (baseball bat and sharp knives kept under mattress)

CHAPTER 6

Contact Between Siblings

One important aspect of this study was to examine the difficulties that occur when contact is maintained between siblings who have experienced an abusive childhood. However, some adopters and foster carers were eager to talk about the severance rather than the maintenance of sibling contact because of its traumatic effects on the child and on the stability of the placement. In the Bilson and Barker research study (1993) they express concern about lost contact for children with siblings elsewhere in the care system. They acknowledge the practical difficulties for busy under-resourced social workers in maintaining contact between siblings. They recommend giving siblings each other's addresses and telephone numbers and helping them to plan visits themselves. The evidence from the present study does not endorse such a recommendation. It clearly demonstrates that when children's background histories have been deeply abusive that contact between siblings needs to be carefully planned, with clarity about the boundaries surrounding the contact relationship, adequately monitored and fully supported. The availability of a third party to offer advice and counsel when difficulties emerge is essential to prevent problems between the different parties who have a high emotional investment in the process escalating out of control.

Seventy-nine children, including 65 adoption and 14 fostering placements, had retained contact with one or more siblings since placement. Twenty-two children had lost at least one of these sibling contacts by the time this study took place. While some had adjusted to this, a small group of six were deeply traumatised through this loss. One eight-year-old boy talked incessantly to his adopters about his brother's loss, waited daily by the letter box yearning for some correspondence from him, and would spend tearful hours staring at his brother's photograph. On many occasions after a temper tantrum had subsided he would tell his adopters that he was sad and angry because he had lost his brother.

Thirty-nine children retained contact with one special sibling while others saw two, three or four siblings who were frequently living in widely scattered geographical areas. Fahad (14) boasted about seeing seven of his eleven brothers. However, retaining contact with such a large number was exceptional. Some children saw their siblings alone; others saw them alongside other adult birth relatives. In the absence of clear planning, some siblings attended contact meetings because it suited the birth parent's convenience rather than because this relationship held any special significance for the adopted child. It was noticeable that when the siblings had not lived together prior to placement, each seemed overtly indifferent towards the other. Sean (11) described his younger brother who was born after he left the family as 'a bit of a brother'.

Nine children with whom contact was being maintained experienced one or more placement disruptions. It took a lot of sensitivity and perseverance to retain links through these troubled times. Adopters and foster carers who were most committed to retaining contact despite these impediments were those who had personal experience of broken family relationships during their own childhood and who knew firsthand how enormous a loss that had been for them.

Siblings with whom contact was maintained. Where did they live?

In adoptive family	In foster family	With birth relative	In independent or semi-independent living	In prison or a young offender's institute
47	26	21	13	2

Figure 13: Siblings with whom contact was maintained. Where did they live?

- 47 (43 per cent) lived with an adoptive family
- 26 (24 per cent) lived with a foster family
- 21 (19 per cent) lived with a birth relative:
  - 10 with both birth parents
  - 9 with birth mother
  - 1 with birth father
  - 1 with grandfather

  (all the children who retained contact with a sibling in this group were in adoption placements)
- 13 (12 per cent) lived independently or semi-independently (women's refuge, sheltered accommodation)
- 2 (2 per cent) lived in prison or in a young offender's institute

The Purpose of Sibling Contact

There were three main reasons why children wanted contact with their siblings.

1. The existence of a strong emotional bond

A deep emotional attachment existed between some siblings. These bonds had been forged when they had lived together during a traumatic childhood. The strength of this bond was most prominently displayed when the sibling relationship was severed. Some children were described as 'pining' for their sibling while others regressed or displayed angry behaviour patterns that adopters and foster carers described as directly attributable to the loss of a cherished sibling. When it was not feasible for contact to be renewed these negative behaviour patterns could be protracted over many months.

2. Concern for the safety of a sibling

Many children wanted to see their siblings as a way of reassuring themselves that they were safe and well. Verbal reassurances seemed to be quite inadequate. Perhaps that is not surprising because the words of adults had often not proved to be trustworthy in the past. Deep concerns were expressed when a new baby was born to the birth parents or when a sibling moved on to a new placement. Face-to-face contact assuaged anxiety and allowed the child to calm down and resume normal living again.

3. The child's need to assume a parental role for a sibling

Life in a dysfunctional family had frequently resulted in roles and relationships being seriously distorted. The burden of parenting other children often rested on the shoulders of a child. Older siblings often took on a protective role for younger ones that extended far beyond a level appropriate to their chronological age. These children found it difficult to relinquish control and continued to have an intense need to protect other children in the family long after they had moved out of their dangerous birth family. The child who had assumed the parenting role while living in the birth family continued to be very vulnerable. One minute this child was trying to function like an over-concerned parent and the next moment like a very immature toddler whose own childlike needs had never been fully met.

Rushton et al. (2001) refer to this issue of 'parentification' in their study of 72 families with siblings in permanent placement. They highlight that this was usually a problem for one child, frequently the eldest in a sibling group, and often a girl. The following quotation from the Rushton et al. research study indicates the short-lived nature of the problem. This quotation contrasts quite markedly with what was happening in this study:

> The 'parentified' child adopted a quasi-parental role, undertaking both nurturing and discipline responsibilities with the younger children to a greater extent than is true of most older children. This behaviour was a common source of concern to parents in the early months. They found it difficult to work out how best to help the child relinquish the role without losing self-esteem, and to establish their own role as parent. However, this problem was relatively short lived in most cases indicating that, despite the difficulties, most of the parents found ways of doing this successfully.

It is worth reflecting on why this problem diminished so quickly in permanent placements of siblings while it persisted as an ongoing problem in contact relationships between siblings. It is possible that it was much easier for adopters and foster carers to address this issue with siblings when they were living together, than with siblings who only saw each other a few times annually at contact meetings.

Barriers to Sibling Contact

Impediments by birth parents

When a sibling lived with a birth parent and the contact arrangement was voluntary, the birth parent's attitude played a significant part in determining the quality of contact. Many birth parents were immature people whose own childhoods had been very deprived. Some were jealous of their child being able to form a close relationship with a sibling. When Sam (8) was placed for adoption it was planned that he would continue to see his brother Kieran (10) during each school holiday. Kieran lived with his birth mother and all the contact arrangements were co-ordinated by social services. Sam loved to see his brother. Whenever they met they wrapped themselves around each other physically and talked and played together as if they had never been apart. After several months Kieran's name was removed from The Child Protection Register and consequently statutory involvement with the birth family ceased. The mother immediately refused access to social workers and banned Kieran from seeing his brother. Sam's devastation was obvious.

Kieran was always on Sam's mind and he talked about him all the time. Stopping contact exacerbated Sam's behavioural problems. He regressed. He was very insecure. He went back to wearing nappies. It usually took a crisis to get him to talk. He'd say that he was upset because of losing Kieran. He even wrote a letter to the social worker saying, 'Get me in touch with Kieran'. Social services have said that it's a closed issue and that it will have to wait until Sam is 18.

Abel (13) always saw his sister Hannah (10) at the same time as he saw his birth mother. Contact with his birth mother was moderately important to him but contact with Hannah meant everything to him. Prior to his most recent contact the birth mother imposed a sanction on Hannah. She was not to talk to her brother. The birth mother found the closeness of Hannah and Abel's relationship hard to tolerate and was eager to keep the focus of attention on herself. After the last contact meeting Abel shed tears of frustration.

If my birth mum doesn't stop playing the game she can sod it.

Impediments by adopters

Some adopters said No to sibling contact. They feared that contact might trigger unmanageable behavioural problems when they were already struggling to cope. Some adopters wanted to block out the reality of adoption and pretend that their adopted child was their own. Others dreaded sexual feelings between siblings being reawakened. One adopter said that she was worried that older siblings might recount memories of sexual abuse and that this might alarm the younger ones. Another had been hesitant because she had read a book that stated that adopted siblings might be sexually attracted towards each other. This adopter had become alarmed after reading a professional paper by Fitsell (1992) about the phenomenon of Genetic Sexual Attraction. Although her concerns were understandable, if she had studied the subject more fully she would have been reassured to discover that when Genetic Sexual Attraction did occur it was a feature associated with sudden reunions in adoption. Such reunions had not been carefully planned with the safeguards associated with thorough preparation, independent counselling and adequate support.

When two or more sets of adopters or foster carers did embark on a contact plan between siblings with some degree of commitment, it was easy for relationships between the different families to break down. When this did happen it was very difficult for contact between siblings to progress satisfactorily. There is an example in this study of how escalating tensions between two adoptive families seriously impeded sibling contact to the point where it was no longer feasible for the siblings to meet. Adopters had different values and diametrically opposed attitudes to parenting. Intense feelings of anger and jealousy between the siblings were also being re-enacted between the adopters. When the adopters began swearing at each other during telephone calls it is not surprising that the children mimicked them.

One social worker summed up the dilemma facing social workers by saying:

> *We do try to make compatible matches between adopters but at the same time we want to place very difficult children. Sometimes adopters are just not on the same wavelength. We have seen again and again how much that spoils contact plans for siblings.*

Impediments by social workers

Changes of social worker sometimes had a profound impact on the implementation and maintenance of contact plans. One adoptive family described how their social services social worker decided to terminate the contact plan when she was leaving because of inadequate resources. She simply stated:

> *I think the time has come to stop contact meetings because the girls have their own lives now.*

Another family who had to relate to a different social services social worker at each contact meeting felt belittled by the impersonal nature of the service available to them.

Nobody in social services knows our son. It feels like he's a 'locked away file'.

In all placements organised by voluntary agencies it was vital that a positive partnership could be established with the social services department responsible for the child. Tensions escalated when social services departments failed to complete essential work and there did not seem to be any way of ensuring that outstanding work would be finished within meaningful timescales. A senior member of staff in a voluntary agency described the dilemma:

Each time we try to discuss the problems we're talking to a new social worker who asks for time to settle in to the job and read the case file. Life Story work has never been done. Social services even have difficulty providing a ten-line contact agreement.

Impediments by children

Some children reached a stage where they decided to opt out of sibling contact. Darren (14) had regular contact with his brother Ben (12) over several years. Gradually they had drifted apart. Darren's adopters had provided him with an affluent lifestyle and opened up exciting opportunities for him. He travelled abroad and developed a fanaticism about playing rugby. Meanwhile Ben's life had stood still. He had continued to live with his birth mother who struggled financially on a meagre state benefit. Although Darren felt guilty because he had everything and Ben had nothing he decided after a lot of heart searching to break the bond. Ben's devastation was obvious to everyone. A few days after being informed of Darren's decision he was found crying by his class teacher. Through counselling he is learning to cope without Darren.

Connor (12) decided for very different reasons to stop seeing his three siblings. Every time he saw them painful memories flooded his mind. He had flashbacks about his birth mother's sadness when she was depressed and of her repeated suicide attempts. His attempts to eradicate memories of being sexually abused by his parents, grandparents and a network of other people seemed to be futile. He has decided that it is impossible to face the future unless he breaks all connections with his siblings.

The Contact Venue

Many families complained about how difficult it was to find a suitable local contact venue (see Figure 14 and following table). Some said that a list of options would have been useful. They felt as if they were experimenting with different venues and hoping against hope that they had made an appropriate choice. Others took the simplest option and used their own home but later regretted that they had not thought more fully about the implications of this.

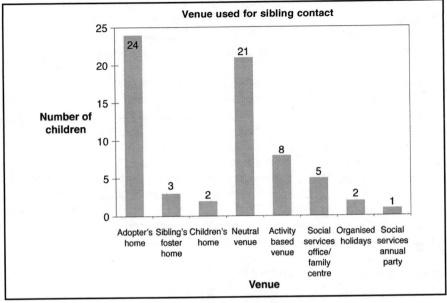

Figure 14: Venue used for sibling contact

Neutral venue	Activity based venue	Organised holiday
Half-way meeting point	Safari park	Adoption UK holiday
Caravan sited in adopter's area	Swing park	Butlins holiday
Airport viewing area	Zoo	
Town centre	Leisure centre	
Garden centre	Swimming	
MacDonalds	Ice-skating	
Charlie Chalk's Restaurants	Bowling	
	Football	
	Cinema	
	Shopping	
	Motor show	

The Advantages and Disadvantages of Using Different Venues

Adopter's home or adopter's geographical location

When an adopter's or foster carer's home was used for sibling contact there was often a power imbalance. The party whose home was being used was often in a superior position and able to exert undue control over events. When tensions already lurked beneath the surface between the adults it was easy for these stresses to escalate and adversely affect sibling contact.

Children could be sensitive to a power imbalance too when the venue was familiar to one sibling and unfamiliar to the other.

The only time that contact didn't work was when we went to the skating rink in the sister's local area. She kept meeting her friends. Philip (12) didn't like that. It made him feel on the outside. His lack of confidence makes him jealous. Now we go where neither one feels more comfortable than the other.

When the adopter's home was used it was vital to analyse the potential connections between the sibling and abusive birth family members in order to minimise the danger of confidentiality being breached. Monash (11) enjoyed annual contact with his four siblings over three years at a neutral venue under the supervision of social services. Sally (16) his eldest sister is in foster care. She has asked if she can visit Monash in his adoptive home. Monash is very excited at this prospect but his adopters are concerned. They know that Sally sees her birth mother. Her birth mother is also in touch with a much wider extended family. Many have been perpetrators of abuse. It is clear that using the adopter's home does have serious long-term implications for Monash's safety.

Overnight stays or holidays

One or two families arranged for children to stay in their sibling's foster or adoptive home overnight or for several days. This could work well. One adoptive couple who had adopted two children and who owned their own hotel offered the adoptive families of the other four siblings a free holiday at their hotel. Their adopted children proudly hosted this occasion and described it as 'brilliant'. An annual holiday arranged by Adoption UK was also a good forum for siblings to meet.

Flexibility in relation to venue

Occasionally a particular venue was suitable initially but the children could quickly outgrow it. In one situation social services had arranged annual contact, between five siblings ranging in age from 4 to 11 years. The contact arrangement extended over six years but the venue remained unchanged and the same toys were produced on each occasion. No attempt had been made to adapt the venue to meet the sibling's changing needs. The adopters described the venue as 'frozen'.

The children's views about venue

The children who participated in the study stressed the importance of using a 'fun' venue where there were interesting activities. Edwin (9) had definite views:

I don't think that it should be in a boring, sitting-down, social services office. I like going to the Zoo or a sports centre.

In contrast Debra (18) who had frequently met her siblings at social services officer had some happy memories associated with this:

I liked being able to muck around with social service's phones because I've always wanted to work in an office.
Other locations that were popular with children were eating burgers at MacDonalds; playing hide and seek; a dinosaur museum; a special shopping centre; playing in the snow and making my brother the wheelbarrow; bowling and swimming; watching a parade; playing our computer games; and staying in holiday cabins. A number of children recommended that a leisure centre should always be the first choice rather than the formality of an office.

Written contact agreements

Written contact agreements were noticeably absent. They were only drawn up in relation to sibling contact for seven of the 65 children in adoption placements. In situations where one sibling remained in the care of a birth parent, the latter was usually unwilling to sign any type of written agreement. Some adopters who experienced contact arrangements degenerating into chaos found it hard to conceal their bitter feelings about relationships that had begun well and terminated in acrimony. These families were the strongest advocates of written agreements.

If we had had something in writing the other adopters wouldn't have been able to back out. It would have prevented serious misunder-standings when our ideas became totally different. The children had the right to expect contact with their siblings but that was destroyed.

Foster carers were more likely to have received some written information about contact arrangements through having access to the minutes of review meetings. However, the information was often scant and included a few sentences about contact rather than a clear detailed plan.

Frequency of Contact

The frequency of contact between siblings varied considerably. Geographical distance between siblings was a major factor that influenced what was feasible rather than the emotional impact following contact. This was markedly different to birth parent contact that often had to be reduced because of its emotional aftermath.

It was not a good idea to begin the contact arrangement with a completely open plan left solely between the different parties to arrange. Relationships that looked straightforward could become amazingly complex. It worked best when:

- There were clear boundaries set.
- There was a structured plan.
- There was an independent person available to advise when difficulties arose.

As contact became more established and as difficulties got sorted out a much more flexible open arrangement for contact could emerge.

A child's wish for sibling contact frequently changed as the placement progressed. This was different to a child's need for birth parent contact that was much more likely to remain consistent unless a very negative or very positive episode occurred that dramatically altered the child's perception. Several adopters described their child's attitude to sibling contact in the following way:

It's much less important now than it was at the start.

Siblings placed in different types of families often grew apart, developed different interests and acquired a new extended family network. It is understandable that children who were placed in a family with no other children were much more likely to retain their enthusiasm about seeing their birth sibling.

However, it was also clear through discussion with at least one teenager that although interest in contact might wane for a period it could revive. Rhata (17) an Asian teenager, is adopted. She has maintained contact with five siblings who have continued to live with her birth parents. She was thoughtful as she reflected on how she thought contact would work out in the future with her birth relatives. This example highlights how contact relationships may need to change throughout different phases of an adoption placement.

Over the next few years I feel that I need space from my birth family to grow up. I think contact will get less and less. Perhaps the odd phone call or the odd letter. I do want to keep in contact with them but I don't want it to be something that I feel I have to do. It's all a bit confusing.

When I'm in my 30s I think it'll increase. I'd want my brothers and sisters to come to my wedding. I'd want to send them pictures of my children and I. My sisters will be married soon. I'd want to go to their weddings and meet their children. I'd want my children to meet their birth relatives. It'll be confusing for them but they should know about it.

Positive Aspects of Contact Between Siblings

Many sibling relationships were marked by good interaction, appropriate physical affection, and an ability to play and talk together. In some instances this involved talking about past traumas. Some looked 'like peas in a pod', behaved alike and 'slotted back together as if they had never been apart'. One adoptive couple who had worked hard to achieve a long term relationship between six siblings felt that the term 'contact' was too harsh and impersonal. They boasted that all the siblings felt like their extended family.

For some children the uniqueness of the sibling bond was more than just a strong blood tie because it was rooted in trauma. Many siblings had survived abusive family experiences together and consequently there was an unspoken empathy between them. Kevin (9) looked up to his older brother. He was adamant that he was the only one that really understood him. One adopter attributed the deep distress of his adopted son Noel (7) at not being able to live with his brother, to the fact that:

They had had a childhood that had been so cocooned in trauma.

Position in the birth family was vitally important to a child like Amy (7). Her adoptive mother explained:

A lot of her identity was tied up with being the big sister.

Through regular contact with her younger brothers Amy was able to derive security through continuing to be the eldest sister.

Melanie (18) and Chloe (17) have been with their adoptive family for five years. They described how their relationship with their birth parents and extended family had disintegrated due to paedophilia. Chloe disdained her birth parents.

I just want to know when they're dead. A cloud will lift off me then.

The fact that Melanie and Chloe had been able to keep in regular contact with their four siblings since joining their adoptive family was a real compensation. There was an element of healing in it. It had been important to salvage something positive from the wreckage of their family life.

Dominic (8) had a history of physical and sexual abuse that had left him deeply damaged. His learning had been impeded and he was unable to establish friendships with other children. His adopters had been amazed at his capacity to form a close relationship with his older brother Luke who is also adopted. Due to distance between the adopters contact involved an overnight stay. Luke and Dominic played and chattered together. Dominic loved it when Luke lulled him to sleep. The most amazing aspect of this contact was that Dominic was totally unable to sustain a calm relationship with any other child for more than a few minutes.

Siblings were able to fill gaps in a child's knowledge or rectify misapprehensions about birth family life. It could be difficult for adopters to eradicate some children's fantasies.

Jason (8) believed that he had seen a witch's face at the window of his birth parent's house. I tried lots of ideas to break down his concerns. I used to say to him, 'Maybe it was the type of glass' but he was never 100% convinced by anything that we said.

At one of the contact meetings I asked the sisters if they remembered any funny stories from their childhood. His sister Cheryl (16) said, 'I remember doing something horrible to Jason. I was holding him and looking up at the house. I told him that there was a witch's face at the window but there was nothing there'.

That was a wonderful thing for her to tell him. The difference that it has made to him has been unbelievable.

A degree of pathos underpinned some sibling relationships. James (13) has two sisters Beth (10) and Pamela (6) who live with their birth mother. Pamela is not important to James. She was born after he left his birth family and it is hard for him to think of her as a real sister. Beth is crucially important to him. His adopter believes that the strength of this bond is because James spent so much of his childhood trying to protect Beth from the abuse that he suffered.

James adores Beth. He says, 'I need to see my sister'. He's got her photo up in his bedroom. When my partner's boy said she looked ugly he punched him. Every week James puts some of his pocket money aside for Beth. When we go to a shop he always asks to buy something for her. James likes designer gear. He looks at his sister with a frilly blouse over her skirt and he worries about her being bullied at Senior School. When he gives her money he tells her what clothes she should buy. He's a grown up in a boy's body.

After James meets his sister sad memories are always revived for him. He recounts incidents to his adoptive mother about childhood beatings, about being forced to eat scraps of food from the bin and about being threatened if he disclosed sexual abuse. James contrasts his sister's quality of life with his own and in a very mature way is able to say a special 'Thank you' to his adoring adoptive mother.

A sibling could be brutally honest about the birth family while the adoptive parents preferred to speak in euphemisms.

At one point Leon (9) said to me, 'I'm not calling them Mum and Dad'. I kept saying to him, 'But they are your parents'. His older sister butted in and said to me, 'Come off it. They're bloody awful parents'.

Occasionally an older sibling had faced disappointment through trying to trace birth parents. Younger siblings listened intently to their experiences and were ready to heed advice about not making the same mistakes. Other siblings began to plan joint strategies for tracing birth parents in the future. This kind of dialogue reduced isolation and made the prospect of searching for abusive birth parents less daunting.

Difficulties

Loss of contact

A small number of children were deeply traumatised through the loss of contact with a sibling. Their level of distress profoundly affected their ability to settle in the placement. Adopters expressed frustration because they often felt that contact with a sibling was in their child's best interests but they were totally powerless to facilitate it. Mary (11) has struggled to accept social services decision that she should not see her brother Joe (9) who is also adopted. When Mary goes through a low period she always talks about how angry she feels about losing Joe.

Mary and her brother Joe have been split since Mary was three years old. When they lived together in the birth family and he screamed she joined in. She dominated him. She felt that she had to mother him. She saw herself as his protector.

We've been advised by social services that it's not in Mary's best interests to have contact with Joe. As far as she's concerned this little person has been taken from her and she's deeply upset.

We're sitting on a time bomb with Mary. In her teens she's going to explode about it. She knows that it's the adults' decision but she's very angry at social services.

New names

Several children became unbelievably distressed when they discovered that an adoptive family had changed a sibling's first name or added a new middle name. Brian (10) flew into an uncontrollable rage when he heard his baby brother's adopters refer to him by the name that they had chosen at his christening. He pleaded with them to revert to his original name. The older sisters of Gina (7) and Karen (5) were indignant when they discovered that their sisters had acquired new middle names.

Repetition of negative patterns in sibling relationships

Some children had been unsuccessfully placed on a short-term basis with one or more siblings prior to their permanent placement. Other siblings had been placed together with a view to permanence but the placement had subsequently disrupted. Common reasons for sibling placements not working out were:

- Problems associated with one sibling dominating the other, making it especially difficult for the more vulnerable child to thrive.
- Sexualised behaviour between siblings.
- Intense rivalry, very demanding behaviour problems and aggression being perpetrated making it difficult for the adopters or foster carers to meet the children's individual needs.

It was interesting to observe how frequently these negative patterns re-emerged when face-to-face contact occurred between siblings. Some families talked about how children regressed and began to exhibit immature behaviour patterns that they assumed had disappeared from their everyday repertoire.

Tony (9) had an older sister Josie, who wanted to control him. She was just continuing what had been so difficult during the placement. She controlled his every move. She took on the mother's role. It was a bit like the Old King's jester. He became her jester and I hated it. Domination had been a feature of the disruption. It became an ongoing saga in contact.

Sexualised behaviour and sexual abuse

Many children had been sexually abused within their birth family. Some were part of a familial paedophile network. One aspect of the abuse was that children were taught to engage in sexual activities with their brothers and sisters. The original decision to split some siblings was connected with the level of sexual activity occurring between them. In seven cases, children engaged in a sexual incident with a sibling during a contact meeting. In four of these, a sexual incident resulted in sibling contact being terminated. In a further six cases the risk of sexual abuse occurring during contact was very high and extreme vigilance was required by adults to monitor sibling behaviour.

As adoptees grew up and took more and more responsibility for their own contact arrangements with siblings a number of adopters worried about how vulnerable the young person was to sexual exploitation.

We do feel that there are risks and some grave concerns for Debra (18). One of the brothers was sexually abusing her when they were in the children's home together. He also sexually abused children in his foster home. She wants to stay at the brother's flat. I've said 'No'. A lot of his relationship with her is sickly and sexual. Another brother was a rent boy in a paedophile ring. The birth mother encouraged that. I'm not sure about her relationship with him. One time she skipped off school and didn't tell us. She was at the brother's flat.

Different stages of coming to terms with the past

Some children wanted to grasp every opportunity to compare notes with a sibling about what had happened during childhood, while the other sibling wanted to close off all conversation because the memories were too painful or even sordid. This could be disappointing for one and very stressful for the other. When Phil (13) discovered that he was going to meet his birth sister Zara (14) his hopes were high. Family ties were all-important to him and he had not seen Zara for seven years. They each had different memories about life with the birth family and they had a history of several years to talk about. Zara could not talk about it. She found it much too disturbing. In order for Phil's relationship with Zara to survive, his adoptive mother had to help him to demonstrate sensitivity towards Zara's wish to block out her feelings.

Unequal benefits: whose needs take priority?

When one child involved in contact arrangements remained in the care of social services there was a tendency for that child's contact needs to take priority over the other siblings who were in adoptive families. Some adopters felt frustrated by the fact that all the power lay with the statutory authority while they were rendered impotent in the decision making process. Tony (7) was originally placed for adoption with his sister Kayley (10). After eight months Kayley's adoption placement disrupted and she returned to her previous foster carers. Regular contact between both siblings was what Kayley wanted. Social services insisted that Kayley's wishes be implemented even though it quickly became apparent that the retention of this sibling relationship was too stressful for Tony. During the week he was facing the possibility of being excluded from school. At weekends when he met his sister he felt belittled and frightened. Tony's single parent adopter felt intimidated by social services especially as they had murmured about taking matters to Court if she was unwilling to comply with the contact arrangements. Although she was convinced that the contact plan was not in Tony's best interests she decided that it was best to wait until an Adoption Order was granted before enforcing her viewpoint. Immediately after adoption she stopped contact for six months to give Tony time to recover. Reflecting on her own experience she raised the question:

What happens if what's best for one child isn't right for the other?

Stan (12), Craig (11) and Marian (9) are siblings who have been placed in different families. Craig is in long term foster care while the other two are adopted. Their birth mother has had a new baby. Social services have instigated Child Protection proceedings because of serious concerns about the welfare of the baby. Social services insist that the new baby has rights. They feel that all the children should see their new baby brother. Stan and Marian's adopters have a different view. They feel that this will merely add an unnecessary burden to their children. Marian has already bombarded her adopters with questions that demonstrate her anxiety about this new baby. The birth of the baby has also aroused angry feelings because of her own rejection.

Who's giving the baby a bottle? Who's changing his nappy? Why is it right for this baby to live with my mum when she didn't keep the rest of us? Are you telling me that one child is alright for her but three is no use. She should just have had Stan then.

Stan and Marian's adopters know that if social services arrange for Craig to see the new baby that they will feel pressurised into allowing Stan and Marian to do the same whether they consider it to be in their best interests or not. Craig would take great delight in boasting to Stan and Marian about having seen his baby brother and intense rivalry between the siblings would have a de-stabilising effect on Stan and Marian's placement.

Confidentiality

Confidentiality was sometimes threatened through sibling contact. After joining his adoptive family Michael (11) had annual contact with his sister Stacey (14). They always met at a social services office. During their last meeting Stacey whispered to Michael, 'Do you think we could meet after this at your house?' Nobody in Michael's birth family had ever visited his adoptive home and he was eager to show off his home and his pet dog. However, Michael's adoptive parents had serious reservations because Stacey sees her birth mother. Three older brothers who were originally implicated in Michael's abuse also keep in contact by telephone with the birth mother.

When Debra (12) gave her adoptive parent's address to her older brothers she did not stop to think about the implications of what she had done. She panicked when she realised that she had opened up the possibility of her irate birth father finding her. He had been writing letters to her adoptive parents that they described as 'crazy and menacing'.

There were one or two isolated incidents where siblings who had been placed reasonably close to each other geographically just happened to meet each other accidentally and this opened up all kinds of unforeseen and sometimes sinister family connections.

Chaotic contact: where are the boundaries?

Without clear planning and firm boundaries surrounding the contact plan it was possible for contact to degenerate into chaos with adopters fighting and children acting out infantile patterns of behaviour. One placement of three deeply damaged siblings who were placed in separate adoptive families with an open ended contact plan is a clear example of this.

Sonia (13), Alison (12) and Colin (11) had been deeply damaged by a very abusive birth mother who was addicted to alcohol and drugs during her pregnancies. The family members were all involved in a complex collusive web of sexual abuse. Colin was described as 'a loner' who 'frequently retreated into his own world'. Alison seemed very insecure with no inner confidence. Sonia had overwhelming needs and swung from being clinging and babyish to aggressive outbursts. Publicity for the children resulted in each of the children being placed in a separate adoptive family. The children loved and hated each other at the same time. There was never any question about terminating contact between the siblings. After placement the question of exactly how much contact would occur was left as an open-ended question that would be determined by the adopters and the children.

The relationship between the adopters quickly deteriorated. The children opened up and closed down contact with their siblings depending on their whim of the day. As tensions escalated the adopters argued with each other, swearing openly in front of the children while the children fabricated tales that threw everyone into a panic. When Alison used her mobile telephone to speak to Colin after months of sullen silence he became so alarmed that he dialled 999. One child vied with another for adult attention. When Sonia cut her wrists, Alison alleged that she had been raped, while Colin instigated police activity when he disappeared overnight. With time to reflect the social worker gave her considered opinion about professional practice.

Looking back I think that we were naïve. What we knew about the birth family's history and their relationships should have enabled us to predict the complexity of it. It was too optimistic to simply think that everyone would get on. The children had very different needs at different times. The birth family's dysfunction got absorbed into the current adopters' relationships. It took a huge crisis for this agency to decide that it needed to take a much firmer pro-active role.

Attempts to establish ongoing contact that floundered

A small group of children could not cope with the stress associated with retaining links with their siblings even though in theory they were committed to it. Terminating contact even after a disastrous contact meeting often evoked ambivalent feelings.

Anne was 12 years old when she was placed for adoption. She had lived with her brother Louis (16) in two different foster placements and had alleged that he had perpetrated sexual abuse combined with a number of cruel rituals. Although she was frightened of him she also felt responsible for him. She felt guilty when he wrote to her saying:

You're my only sister. I don't want to lose you.

After six months he asked to see her. Although Anne was hesitant she decided to say 'Yes'. The encounter proved to be much harder than Anne had anticipated. It triggered all kinds of conflicting emotions from the past. The aftermath was frightening for herself and everyone else who was close to her as she exhibited destructive and sexualised behaviour. Following this her adopters helped her to compose a letter to Louis saying that she did not want to see him again.

However, this chapter in her life is not completely closed. Eighteen months after the meeting with her brother her adoption placement disrupted. Anne has now said that she wants to see Louis again.

Ben was placed for adoption at 11 years of age. He was massively withdrawn and virtually mute. His sister Tara (15) who has learning difficulties was placed with another adoptive family. Ben and Tara had been together in residential care. Tara had displayed very sexualised behaviour towards Ben and he had been very rejecting of her. It was always planned that there would be face-to-face contact between them several times a year but that careful monitoring would be essential. After travelling many miles to see Tara it was immediately apparent that this type of contact was not going to work.

Ben had a strong fear reaction, sticking close to his adopters. Tara's severe learning difficulties made her move and relate awkwardly. She was big and boisterous and kept grabbing hold of him. He was uncomfortable. It was unsettling and frightening for him. He couldn't cope. It brought up the past. He wanted to close that down. He hated reminders about it.

After this meeting Ben was completely resistant to seeing Tara again.

Having spent fifteen months trying to promote contact between three siblings, who had been respectively twelve years, nine years and seven years in separate adoptive and foster families, one social services social worker could not hide her disappointment about her limited success:

> *Despite all our work the best we've achieved has been hit-and-miss contact. The level of abuse from parents and the level of abuse towards each other has resulted in contact being detrimental to the children. The placements were full of crises and the crises about contact became embroiled in that.*

> *We hoped that if we provided pleasant surroundings and interesting activities that it would help the siblings to think positively about each other but it has always evoked memories from the past and has had a disturbing effect.*

> *I'd say that the following factors have prevented it from working:*
> - *Distance.*
> - *Negative relationships between adopters.*
> - *A reluctance on the part of the adopters because of what it raises for the children.*
> - *The high level of monitoring required to prevent sexualised behaviour between siblings occurring.*

After Disruption: Rushed Contact

Four children who were placed on a permanent basis with their siblings experienced disruption of their placement. They had to move out of their family while their sibling remained. In each of these cases social workers advocated with unmitigated zeal that immediate contact be retained between siblings. Expectations about the level of contact that was essential were very high. In two cases weekly contact was proposed. Besides, there was a high expectation that the adopters who were just emerging from the experience of disruption should attend all contact meetings. In two cases the adopters were told that the other child might be removed if they were unwilling to comply with the contact plan.

Each of these situations was fraught with difficulty. Adopters seemed uncommitted by failing to confirm dates or providing a weak excuse for not attending. Even more worrying there was clear evidence in one case of an open rejection and even a hatred of the child. One social worker said:

> *The adopters who had lived through disruption saw him as evil and they wanted to punish him.*

Another adopter made a false promise to the child about returning to live with them if behaviour improved. Others were so numbed by the experience of disruption that it proved impossible for them to allow the siblings who remained in placement to express emotions associated with loss.

It is worth asking the question; 'Was such rapid contact really essential?' If so, this is one situation where the adopters needed time to recover from disruption first. It might have been better if they had been allowed to take a back seat for a period in order to allow them to work through the stages of grief associated with bereavement. It was interesting to note that as time elapsed there were marked signs of improved relationships between all the parties as everyone had time to rebuild their lives after a devastating crisis.

An Overview of the Effects on Children of Sibling Contact

Many children benefited from sibling contact and thoroughly enjoyed the experience of being able to spend time with their brothers and sisters. It was clear that the most important sibling was the one with whom they had forged a close bond while living in the birth family. It helped when they could see for themselves that their sibling was thriving. This enabled them to get on with living without becoming over concerned about a sibling's welfare. However, in some situations it was possible for one child to benefit from contact with a sibling while the other one was merely experiencing a repetition of abusive behaviour that had been a reason for placing the siblings separately.

When siblings were placed in very different adoptive families whose lifestyles were culturally and materially different there was a likelihood that the siblings would grow apart. When the adoptive families had similar values and aspirations and could relate well together it was more likely that sibling relationships would endure.

A small group of six children who wanted contact with a sibling to continue but were denied this wish were deeply traumatised. The child who had undertaken an inappropriate parenting role while living in the birth family was most vulnerable when contact with that sibling was severed. A deep-rooted need to continue to protect the sibling was not easily eradicated.

Six children could not cope with the reality of contact with a sibling even though they were committed to it. It raised too many unresolved feelings associated with the abuse that they had suffered.

When a sibling placement disrupted for one child and the other remained in placement it was tempting to rush into immediate contact arrangements between the siblings. However, this could be a very damaging experience for the child who had had to leave the family. Adopters were often emotionally disabled by the experience of disruption and therefore unable to facilitate immediate contact. They needed time to grieve first. When this did not happen feelings of shock, anger, denial and sadness could be inappropriately projected on to the child.

Summary of Key Points

- Effect on Children of Sibling Contact

   Most children are likely to derive benefit and enjoyment through sibling contact but a minority of children are liable to find it too stressful because it evokes unresolved painful memories of early trauma.

   The most deeply traumatised children in this study were those who had undertaken a protective role for a sibling while living in the birth family and who found that sibling relationship severed against their wishes.

- Planning

   If sibling contact is going to work well it requires clear planning, the establishment of clear boundaries about, who, where, how often, and what, the availability of a third party to mediate and provide objective advice, and a flexible system that responds to children's changing needs. A written contact agreement is important when so many different parties with competing interests are involved.

   An assessment of the attitudes of all parties involved in contact is essential before embarking on any contact plan. Where one party erects a barrier there are likely to be ongoing difficulties for children.

- Adoptive families' compatibility

   When children are placed with different adoptive families, contact arrangements are most likely to achieve enduring success where families share similar values and find each others' company mutually rewarding. When there are marked differences between adopters in relation to status, class and interests it is much harder for contact to survive on a long-term basis.

- Venue

   A good quality venue is essential and is one way of conveying a non-verbal message to children that their relationship with their birth relatives is valuable. When choosing a venue for sibling contact it is important to take account of the following factors:
   - Children's ages, interests and wishes.
   - Whether the venue is commensurate with the level of monitoring required.
   - A full assessment of the links between the sibling and birth relatives who have previously perpetrated abuse. Does the venue adequately preserve confidentiality and provide protection for

children from previous abusers, not just in the short-term but also in the long-term?

- The need to review the suitability of the venue as children reach different developmental stages and their circumstances alter.

- **Geographical distance between siblings**

  Geographical distance between adoptive families, rather than the emotional aftermath of contact is likely to be the greatest barrier to sibling contact.

- **Re-emergence of previous negative behaviour patterns associated with splitting siblings**

  Difficult behaviour patterns between siblings that led to splitting were liable to resurface during contact meetings and could be deeply damaging. Through an assessment of sibling's previous behaviour patterns it should be feasible to make predictions about behavioural difficulties that are likely to arise in contact meetings and to prepare to manage this.

- **Changed names**

  An adoptive family may choose to change a child's name. Siblings need preparation for this emotive issue prior to a contact meeting.

- **Lack of financial support**

  The absence of a financial budget underpinning contact plans prevented contact plans from being developed fully for some children.

- **Review**

  The review system available to foster children ensured that their contact needs were regularly reviewed. In contrast there was no review system available to adopted children. An appropriate system needs to be developed to ensure that contact plans do not stagnate.

- **Contact after disruption**

  When one sibling's placement disrupts while the other remains in placement, it is unhelpful to expect the adopters who have just emerged from disruption to rush into contact meetings. The adopters are likely to need time to work through the stages of grief that usually occur after such a wounding experience before becoming an integral part of any ongoing contact plan.

CHAPTER 7

The Children's Perspective

Establishing open communication with children and ascertaining their wishes and feelings in relation to decision making about them are hallmarks of good professional practice. A vital aspect of this study was to listen to children and young people's views about contact with their birth relatives. Even though the subject that was being discussed was deeply sensitive it was clear that children were enthusiastic about being consulted. Some said that they were proud to think that their opinions were important enough to be included in a book.

Thirty-seven children and young people aged between five years and 21 years participated. Figure 15 illustrates with whom these 37 children had maintained contact.

Contact with whom?

Birth mother	Birth father	Siblings	Grandparents	Great aunts or uncles	Cousins
15	11	25	5	3	2

(Some children had contact with more than one birth relative.)

Figure 15: Contact with whom?

In all situations the permission of adopters and foster carers to talk with their child was requested. Those who declined to permit their children to be interviewed did so for the following reasons:

- They felt that their child was confused about family relationships and would be unable to grasp the meaning of the questions.
- The child was exhibiting behavioural problems and they were concerned that reviving past memories might exacerbate these difficulties.
- Sensitive issues surrounding contact with the birth family remained unresolved and they felt that the child might be suspicious about the purpose of the research interview.
- One adoptive family stated that they had determined that their children would not be expected to talk to anyone outside the family about their traumatic childhood. They felt that there had been too much intrusion by professionals into the children's private lives in the past.

Interviews with children took place in their own home. Prior to embarking on the interview it was important to negotiate with the adopters about the availability of private space for the interview. This was not always easy. When adopters hovered in the background or appeared and reappeared during the interview it proved to be quite distracting for the child. One adopter insisted on observing the interview. This was very unhelpful as the child constantly looked to the adopter for reassurance and actually asked the adoptive mother to answer some questions. Some adopters asked if they could see their child's work. In these situations children were informed about this request before commencing work and it was the child's decision how much of their work they showed to their adoptive parents.

Some interviews presented the researcher with greater challenges than others. One example was a teenage boy who had serious problems. He had developed a pattern of spending most of his free time isolated in his bedroom in the dark. His foster carers felt that he would be unlikely to manage an interview extending beyond twenty minutes. He did in fact concentrate without any apparent difficulty for more than an hour and talked openly about how devastated he was by his birth parent's rejection. At the conclusion of the interview he made a poignant death wish for his birth mother:

I hope that she dies slowly, painfully and quickly.

It was clear when undertaking the interviews that some children's feelings were very deep which made it painful for them to express how they felt while others appeared to have much more superficial feelings and could talk quite openly. Jenny (10) seemed very cautious about every word that she uttered. Again and again she began to say something important. Suddenly she would hesitate and say, 'I've forgot'. Jenny's foster carers described her 'as a very sad child who kept all her problems inside'. In contrast, her sister Roseanne (9) had no difficulty in articulating some very sad memories associated with birth family life.

Unfulfilled Hopes in Relation to Birth Family Contact

Despite the fact that the 37 children who participated in the study did have contact with at least one birth relative, 20 children expressed a real yearning to see others and a deep sense of disappointment because this had not been feasible (see Figure 16).

In ten instances children described an unfulfilled wish to have contact with a birth parent. In the case of three siblings there was a glimmer of hope that contact with the birth mother might be instigated, following a series of psychotherapeutic sessions. There seemed to be very little prospect of any

Birth mother	Birth father	Sibling	Other birth relatives
8	2	7	3

Number of children = 20.

Figure 16: Additional birth relatives whom children wished to see

of the other children who wanted to see their birth parents having this desire fulfilled. One 13-year-old girl admitted that she had not dared to voice her secret wish to see her birth father to her adoptive parents. Another 21-year-old had ripped up all her birth mother's photographs because of a deep resentment towards her. She had wondered about searching for her but she had decided not to pursue this course of action because she feared rejection. She decided that it was best 'not to drag up the past'.

The seven children who wanted to see additional siblings had usually made some futile efforts to do so. Frequently the sibling's adopters said an outright 'No'.

The other birth relatives with whom contact would have been welcomed were cherished aunts, cousins or grandparents who had played a significant part in the child's early life. As children reminisced about these birth relatives it was clear that they still retained affection for them.

Longing to find out more

Several children described a deep yearning to obtain more information about their birth family, especially their birth parents. Six children talked about not knowing who their birth father was and about how deeply this affected them. Celia (9) drew her birth father's face in question marks indicating that every feature of his physical appearance was an unknown. This was a particularly sensitive issue for her because her older sisters who were placed in the same adoptive family had a different birth father about whom they did have salient information. Rita (13) wondered if she could ask her birth mother whom she saw annually about her birth father. She knew that her birth parents' relationship had been fleeting and she worried that it might make her birth mother 'sad' if she asked for information.

Some children who saw their birth parents did not feel that they knew enough about them. Although Gary's adoptive father said that Gary (10) only concentrated for a few minutes when he saw his birth parents and then ran away to play, Gary said that he longed to know minute details about his birth parent's everyday existence as this would enable him to think about them better.

I wish I knew what's going on in my birth family. What they're doing: if they're going somewhere and if they're getting hurt.

Regina's (14) birth mother had died when she was two years old. She longed to know more about her. She had questioned her birth father but every time she summoned the courage to ask him a basic question about her he diverted the conversation on to another topic.

Feelings and Attitudes Towards the Birth Family

When completing Ben's Story, (see Chapter 2), children had ample opportunity to draw and describe their feelings about their birth family. They were presented with the following feelings in pictorial form and asked which faces fitted their story.

They were then invited to add extra feelings. Later in the questionnaire they were given the following list of words and asked to circle those that depicted their attitude towards contact with their birth relatives.

happy	delighted	weird
confused	nervous	pleased
glad	cheerful	good
guilty	afraid	smiley
excited	bad	worried
angry	upset	

The complexity of feelings associated with contact became evident as children completed these exercises. Many children took a word and inserted ½ beside it and explained that good and bad feelings were happening at the same time. Roseanne (9) did that with a range of words.

happy ½ delighted ½ glad ½ weird ½ good ½

Others partially circled a word and described how the different emotions overlapped, e.g. ⊂happy ⊂sad. Celia (9) drew a face that was happy on one side and angry on the other. Colin (9) dismissed the above words as far too straightforward with the comment, 'I can't put down my words because they would be swear words'.

He then proceeded to invent his own words.

muddly angry (you can't work things out inside)	left out angry
angry angry	*miserable* angry
a mixed up mess	a weird and horrible tummy feeling
uncomfortable	grumpy
	fed-up

He then said that his feelings were like all the colours in the rainbow mixed together. Most of his colourful rainbow emotions were negative but there were occasional glimmers of positive feelings too. The confusing issue was that all the colourful feelings in Colin's rainbow were 'swidged' together.

Some children described the pain associated with trying to work out their turbulent feelings. It was easier to switch off and block out their feelings. Debra (18) said:

In general I'm confused. My whole life is mucked up. I'm mixed up about my birth family. They're strange people. I just try to block it out.

Sean (11) was encouraged to talk openly to his adopters. They recalled that after a sudden outburst of temper he had written on a piece of paper, 'I wish that I felt nothing for my birth father'.

Many children selected the word **confused** and then talked about different reasons for feeling confused.

- Being too young to have memories about what had happened in their birth family and not knowing whether it was possible to trust what people said.
- Finding it too hard to talk about what had happened in the past.
- Finding it difficult to understand why the birth family had decided to relinquish them while caring for other birth children.
- Living between two different worlds with opposing lifestyles and values: the world of the adoptive family and the world of the birth family.
- Hating and loving certain birth family members simultaneously, and being confused by discovering positive feelings for certain family members who had perpetrated sexual abuse.
- Being frightened of saying the wrong thing to a birth relative during contact meetings.
- Ruminating over the question, 'Which family do I love most?'

Children and teenagers then either drew or wrote in some extra words and phrases that described how they felt.

an outsider	apologetic
deep inside feelings	negative
filled with hate	abnormal
clammed up	torn
scared	disappointed
extra cross	curious to know more
depressed and aggressive	nightmarish
jealous of normal people	lonely
stressed	extra cautious
pessimistic	abandoned
disgusted (is it my fault?)	fear of rejection
hurt inside	crying
always thinking about what happened in the past	

Children's feelings about the importance of expressing painful emotions

Children and young people talked about how difficult it was to express their innermost feelings. One adoptive family had explained during their research interview how William (16) had 'just switched off' when his birth mother refused to have further contact with him. During William's interview he confirmed how hard it had been for him to talk.

> *I found it very hard opening up to my adoptive family. I couldn't talk to them but when I did I found that I got a positive reaction. I've learned that it's better to open up and to say things rather than keeping them inside you. If you do keep it inside, you regret it and then feel down about it.*

When Danny (10) joined his adoptive family at five his emotions were frozen. He could not cry. He told his story in the following way and offered this advice to other adopted children:

> *I was adopted because my family wasn't decent to me. Being adopted aint that bad. It wasn't my fault. It was my parent's fault. Don't get mad with yourself. It doesn't matter if you cry a lot.*

Shane (15) had found therapy helpful at different phases of his adoption placement. After five years with his adoptive family he is gradually finding ways of controlling his aggressive outbursts. He offered advice to other adopted children:

> *If you feel angry and upset don't hold it in. Things get better with time.*

Attitudes to Contact with Birth Relatives

Attitudes to birth parent contact

Children's attitudes to contact with their birth parents were remarkably diverse. Some children clearly had a huge emotional investment in the relationship. Others had no real affection for their birth parents but they needed to know that they were safe and well. Some had a need to rehearse firsthand with their birth parents the story of their life while others wanted to obtain factual information and to learn more about themselves by finding out about inherited traits. It was not possible to observe any particular gender differences affecting these attitudes although it was more common for boys rather than girls to talk about how much they missed their birth father.

Sonia (15) joined her adoptive family when she was nine. While living in her birth family, she had been both physically and sexually abused by a number of male relatives while her birth mother had been unable to protect her. Sonia now has contact with her birth mother on an annual basis. The fact that a strong emotional bond exists between Sonia and her birth mother is something that both Sonia and her adopters readily admit. Sonia feels that face-to-face contact has strengthened that bond, and provided her with tangible evidence that her birth mother still loves her.

Fahad (14) had a birth mother who was a prostitute with an elusive lifestyle. He worried about her and needed the reassurance of knowing that she was safe. His comments about contact are exceptionally positive.

If I was adopted and couldn't see my birth family the gap in my life would be the length of the M25.

Other children were much less positive. Regina (14) said that not seeing her birth father would be a loss but only a small loss. Donna (12) described contact with her birth father as boring and then added 'He even walks funny'. Sean (11) found contact with his birth parents frustrating as they often arrived late, avoided his penetrating questions and rejected social worker's case records about his abusive early history as false. After contact Sean is disappointed and disillusioned. This is how he summed up his feelings:

It's like having an uncle and aunt that you have to go and see, and you don't expect to get much out of it.

Colin (9) had a teenage birth mother. She developed intense short-term relationships with a series of boyfriends. Colin suffered serious physical injuries at the hands of different boyfriends. Colin thinks that one of the good things about having contact with his birth family is, 'That it places the blame where it really belongs'.

Attitudes to sibling contact

Attitudes to sibling contact were also diverse. Paul (21) has learning difficulties. He describes contact with his siblings as brilliant. The only cloud on the horizon for him is a private fear that they might not turn up. Michael (11) is the only child in his adoptive family. Meeting his siblings every year is a very special event that he boasts about at school. He says that it makes him feel perky. Chloe (17) has been able to see her four siblings regularly over the five years that she has been with her adoptive family. That has been quite remarkable because they are all widely scattered geographically. She says that there is a strong bond between them that will last forever.

Occasionally the relationship with a sibling was tense and lacking in trust because there had been abusive episodes in the past. Debra (18) was sexually abused by her brother when she lived with him in a children's home. She would like these incidents to fade into past history but they continue to haunt their relationship.

I wish that my brother would forget the sexual abuse. Part of me hates him. Part of me feels close to him. We get on well. He was 13 years old when he abused me. He suffered abuse by his uncle. He apologises over and over again. I say, 'Forget it. Can we not just get on with life?'

Attitudes to terminated contact

Several children who had had contact terminated with a significant birth relative spoke movingly about their sense of loss. Sam (14) was totally rejected at birth by his mother. At four years old he went into foster care while his older brother John remained with the birth mother. John meant everything to Sam. After being placed for adoption Sam did see John two or three times until his birth mother banned John's visits. Sam wonders whether his birth mother should have been asked to sign a form from the Court to say that John's visits must continue. Sam has not seen John for five years. His loss has felt like a death and he still cries when he thinks about him. He has resolved that as soon as he reaches 18 he will visit the city where John lives and not give up until he finds him.

William (16) has only seen his birth mother twice since he was placed for adoption. His birth mother terminated contact following a sexual incident between William and his siblings. William has one secret wish, 'Bring my birth family back'. He has reacted to his loss by forcing himself to stop thinking about his birth family. He feels that it is the only way that he has managed to survive.

Brendan (15) has also lost all the significant people in his birth family. His birth mother has said 'No' to any opportunity for contact with him. His sister has lived through one disrupted placement after another. Recently he travelled many miles to see her and she failed to appear. His birth father's contact has been very erratic and now he has lost interest, despite countless false promises to visit him. Brendan's sense of rejection has been total. He has been unable to make any close relationships and is frightened of physical affection. Most of his free time he remains very distant from everyone in his foster family. He says that inside him there are 'waves of anger that shake his body up inside'.

The Joys and Difficulties Associated with Contact

The joys

Several children commented on the joy of being able to attend a special occasion like a wedding when all the members of their birth family were present together. It was a rare event for all the birth family to be physically under one roof. A number acknowledged that they felt 'normal' and 'together' when this happened. Even a birth family funeral could have some positive aspects.

> *When my grand-dad died all my brothers came to the family. I was glad that we were in the same room in the same place. It was the first time that had happened.*

Others commented on the happiness associated with members of their adoptive family being able to share in an event with members of their birth family. Sinead (17) recalls one special contact meeting that was a highlight in her calendar.

> *I remember one time that was really good. My cousin from this family who is in his thirties came with me. He's just a big kid. There was he and I and my birth brothers. I was getting on well with my brothers. We were playing snooker and messing about. I was really happy.*

Sharon (17) has similar memories:
> *One time my older brothers from this family came out for a meal with me and my birth mother and her boyfriend. My adoptive parents came too and my grandparents from my birth family. It was really good having them all together. I was so happy.*

Another advantage of birth family contact was that children were less likely to miss out on the birth of a new family member. Debra (18) identified her three-year-old nephew as one of the most special of all her birth family members. Regina (14) was excited about getting to know her half sister's baby.

Difficulties: unrealistic hopes and expectations

Some children had unrealistic expectations about what their birth family could offer. Paul (21) learned through experience to revise his hopes.
> *It was difficult to get love from my birth family. I've never had that. I yearned for it. I clung on to my background. I used to dream that we'd all be together and be a close-knit family. I had to learn not to put too much faith in my birth family. They had their problems as well as me.*

The question of frequency

Most children wanted contact meetings to happen much more frequently than was feasible. This was particularly true at the beginning of their permanent placement. A number voiced deep resentment about not having any sense of control over this issue.

Venue and the importance of confidentiality

The issue of confidentiality was vitally important. A number of children talked about the difficulties associated with contact happening in the birth family area. It was not just that children had troubled memories that were stirred by the geographical location but there were also serious risks of colliding with an abusive family member. Sonia (15) had very real worries about this each time she visited her birth mother.
> *When I was seeing my birth mum last year I was really frightened that my dad would pass the house and that he would get my mum. He does pass the house sometimes when he's going to the shops. I was pleased that my mum has a boyfriend to protect her.*

Tensions between adopters or foster carers and birth relatives

Tensions between the adoptive or foster family and the birth family affected children profoundly. Several teenagers talked about how distressed they were when their adoptive family openly criticised their birth relatives. Gloria (17) decided that the best approach was to close down all conversation about her birth family. This is how she described her dilemma:

My adoptive mother made horrible comments. She tried to drum into my brain how bad my family were. I don't talk to her about my birth family because she's always slagging them off. I keep it to myself. I used to get into real conflict by asking myself, 'Which family do I like best'? I used to get so confused that I decided to leave the question with no answer.

Teenagers found it especially difficult to cope with having a birth parent and an adoptive parent of the same gender present together at contact meetings. This was a recurring theme. The tension associated with this was enormous. Teenagers felt torn in two different directions and often just did not know what to do.

It's a bit confusing having two mums with you. Do you say, 'This is my mum' and then, 'This is my real mum'. You're worried about your real mum. She might get worried that I have another mum. You're worried about your adoptive mum. She might get worried that I have another mum.

Sharon (17) has been in her adoptive family for five years. During this period she has seen her birth mother, grandparents, uncles and aunts and her cousins on a regular basis. Her adoptive parents have found many of these meetings very frustrating. Although Sharon seems keen to see her birth family she becomes withdrawn and almost mute when she is with them. It has only now dawned on Sharon's adopters that they may be placing her in a situation of conflict by being present at each of these meetings and they have decided to withdraw. Their suspicion that Sharon was experiencing torn loyalties was amply evidenced when Sharon shared her views during the research interview.

It's awkward having two mums and two dads. You really don't know which one to talk to. I kept trying to smile at them both. My dad doesn't like my birth mum.

What's It Like Having Two Families?

Older children and teenagers were asked:

If another adopted child said to you, 'What's it like having two families – an adoptive family and a birth family?' what would you say?

This question evoked three main responses:

- I've only one family.
- I'm caught between two very different families.
- It's like an extended family.

'I've only one family'

Some children only considered themselves to have one family and that was their adoptive or foster family. Regina (14) has been living for two years with her permanent foster family. Prior to this she had been in an adoption placement that disrupted. She retains regular contact with her birth father.

> *I only have one family: this foster family. Andy is my dad. Mary is my mum. I know that the facts are that my dad is my birth dad. That's all that's to it: a fact. When I have children I'll want my foster mum to baby sit. I won't turn to my birth family.*

Sean (11) implied that it was too difficult to think about being connected to two families because that reintroduced memories of past hurts.

> *I just think of the one I'm in at the moment. There's nothing to be gained by thinking about your birth family. I only think about them when I have good reason to.*

Melanie (18) and her sister Chloe (17) expressed a complete rejection of their birth parents. Chloe said:

> *I've just got adoptive parents. As far as my birth parents are concerned I'd say with determination that the minute they treated me wrongly they became strangers. I don't consider them as part of my family. My adoptive parents will be my parents for the rest of my life.*

Then Melanie added:

> *If I met my birth father I'd say, 'I hate you. I want to kill you and walk out'.*

'I'm caught between two very different families'

Other children and teenagers felt torn between the worlds of their birth family and their adoptive family. Having two families was described as 'confusing', and 'a bit strange'. One teenager said, 'It's not your normal average thing and you feel odd'.

Tricia (12) felt that she was living between two different cultures. Her birth family originated from a working class area in East London and she felt that it helped her to return to her geographical roots. At the same time she had to fit in with her foster family's middle class ethos where there were different norms and values.

> *I have two very different families. I don't have a choice. I get upset inside but I try not to show it. You just want to be normal. You feel jealous of your friends and you can get quite paranoid.*

Suzy (17) contrasted her foster family from whom she could receive sound advice with her birth family whose only interest in life seemed to be to frequent pubs.

Debra (17) had no hesitation in expressing her view.

> *It's a bit weird having two families. It's mucked up my life. It's not an asset at all to be adopted. I call my adoptive parents by their first names. I don't call them mum and dad because that feels right. You feel that you're caught up in a real conflict.*

'It's like an extended family'

A small number of children said that having two families was just like having an extended family and that it made them feel very special. Fahad (14) said, 'It feels like one big massive family. It's like an extended family'.

When he was asked which family was his main family and which was his extended family he hesitated and said, 'I'm not sure'.

Shane (15) and his sister Rita (14) echoed similar sentiments. Shane said:

It's like an extended family. Both families care for you even if one can't care as well as the other. I see my birth mum as often as I see my nan in my adoptive family so it doesn't feel like another family.

Rita added:

I'm lucky. I know that my birth mum loves me. I know that this family love me. They chose me. They must love Shane and me to go through all that they've been through.

Wishes for the Birth Family

Teenagers and children who were able to respond to the research question-naire were asked:

If you had three wishes for the future about your birth family what would they be?

Younger children were asked a simpler question in pictorial form:

Sometimes Ben imagines that he has a magic wand that he could wave and it would make things different. If you had a magic wand what would you make it do?

Children and young people expressed a strong wish that the negative features of their birth family could be transformed and that they could live with their birth family.

Make time to go back and make my birth parents good parents so I could stay with them. That would make things simpler.

Some talked about a yearning to find a birth parent while others expressed a genuine sadness that they had been denied the ultimate opportunity to see a significant birth relative who had died. Some wished that a sibling with whom no contact was maintained would find out about them and trace their address. Tricia (12) who was in a permanent foster family was adamant that she would return to live with her birth family when she was 18 years old. She hoped that she would be able to live with her birth mother.

Some teenagers had reached the stage of completely rejecting their birth parents. One teenager said that 'a cloud would lift off her when she heard that they were dead'. Brendan (15) said with a degree of defiance that he would like to plant a high explosive bomb close to his birth mother. His foster carers recalled watching him anxiously during a recent holiday as he had stood on the beach staring aimlessly into space and throwing one stone after another into the sea with the aggressive comment, 'This is my mum. This is all women'.

Chloe (17) said tearfully:

I used to want my birth parents to be miserable in prison and to die. Now I want them to grow a heart and to think about what they have done and what they have lost. I want them to look in a mirror and think, 'Why was I such a fraud?' Their mistreating us has meant that they have lost six great kids.

Chloe did not want to complete her interview without paying high tribute to her adoptive family and to social workers who had made crucial decisions on her behalf.

My biggest dream has come true through adoption. It was right for social services to separate us. It was better for each of us to have one-to-one attention. My youngest brother was only two years old when he was taken away and he needed a lot of care, support and love. I wouldn't have liked to keep someone in the family back.

I've got my adoptive mum's personality and my adoptive dad's love of sport. Thank you social services. You have done the best matching that I've ever known.

Is Social Work Supervision Helpful or Unhelpful?

Twenty-three children and young people had some experience of a social worker supervising contact and were able to talk from personal experience about the social worker's role. Three expressed indifference towards the social worker's presence. Eleven were enthusiastic about the social worker being there because 'it made them feel safe', 'it made everything run smoother' and 'it was a good way of keeping things under control'. It obviously made a difference to the child when the social worker knew the child well. Some children spoke enthusiastically about having their favourite social worker at contact meetings.

Teenagers especially liked to use the social worker as an intermediary.

We were like two teams – my adoptive mum and me versus my big birth family and me. The social worker was in the middle. We could communicate through her. It was especially good to have the social worker at the Family Centre at first but it would have been awkward if she'd continued coming when it was in my birth family's house.

A number of teenagers felt strongly that their adoptive parents should not attend contact meetings with their birth parents but it was usually far too sensitive an issue to ask the adoptive parent to opt out. Often there was no alternative. Trying to relate to a birth parent and an adoptive parent simultaneously was too stressful. They preferred to have a neutral person like a social worker alongside them.

I liked having a social worker there. That was better than my adoptive parents.

Suzy (17), who was rather immature for her years lived in a permanent foster family. She felt aggrieved that social work supervision had been withdrawn because of scarce social services' resources. Her birth mother was an alcoholic. They usually met at an agreed venue in the town where Suzy lived. When her birth mother turned up in an inebriated state Suzy had to decide single-handedly how to respond.

Nine expressed a negative attitude towards social work supervision. Regina (14) totally resented her social worker being present when she met her birth father.

I dislike the social worker being there very much. What's it got to do with my social worker? I'm at a stage when I don't want social workers to rule my life.

Others felt that it impeded their relationship with their birth family. It destroyed privacy and spontaneity. When Melanie (18) and her sister Chloe (17) met their siblings they felt stifled and crushed by the level of supervision that social workers provided. It felt like total surveillance that included every move and every word being monitored.

The following factors were helpful in relation to supervision:

- Continuity of social worker.
- Child liking the social worker.
- A system for regularly reviewing the type and level of supervision required so that appropriate amendments could be made.
- Children who were newly placed in their permanent family often needed the security of having an adoptive parent present throughout contact. Teenagers who were more established in their permanent placement could feel 'torn' between their two families when their adopter was present during contact meetings. They often expressed a preference for having a more neutral person like a social worker present.

The following factors were unhelpful in relation to supervision:

- Excessive monitoring leaving the child feeling stifled.
- Having a social worker present with whom the child was unfamiliar.
- Withdrawal of supervision at a stage when the child or young person felt unsafe or unable to cope with the demands or risks associated with seeing the birth family.
- The decision to automatically withdraw supervision at a point when an Adoption Order was granted or when a foster child acquired 18 years was especially unhelpful for children from such impoverished backgrounds, who often needed additional time to mature.

Support

Sources of support about which children had either positive or negative comments to make were:

- Adopters and foster carers.
- Members of the adopters' or foster carers' extended family.
- Social worker.
- Other adopted or foster children.
- Special friends.
- School.

Adopters and foster carers

Children were asked:

> *When you feel mixed up or upset about contact with your birth family who do you turn to?*

It quickly became apparent that adoptive parents and foster carers were the primary source of support. Some children said they were the only people they would confide in. The comment, 'When I talk to my adoptive mum she understands' was typical of the sentiments expressed by many children. Jenny (10) identified her foster carers as the most important people that she turned to when difficulties occurred and then wrote in large letters beside their names '**special**'. Regina (15) complimented her foster carers by saying, 'They know everything. They have brains like Jupiter'.

Only two teenage girls said that they did not feel able to confide in their foster carers or adopters. One was angry because she had been moved to her present foster placement against her wishes. Another 17-year-old talked in detail about how much tension existed between herself and her adoptive mother. She felt aggrieved because her adoptive mother showed clearly that she disapproved of her birth relatives. When the adoptive mother entered the room during the research interview the atmosphere became very tense and the teenager exploded, 'That woman jars my brain'.

Members of the adopters' or foster carers' extended family

Members of the adopters' and foster carers' extended family were a significant source of support. A special aunt, uncle, grandparents or older sons and daughters of the adopters or foster carers were mentioned. However, some members of the extended family were nonplussed about why children needed to keep in contact with their first family.

Social worker

A few children talked positively about their social worker. They thought that it was a good idea to talk with a social worker when difficulties occurred. Rita (15) said, 'My social worker was really good. She helped me'.

Other adopted or foster children

Seven children and young people expressed enthusiasm about the fact that they knew someone in their peer group who had personal experience of adoption or fostering. There were no examples of these connections having been organised by the placing agency. The following quotations illustrate the meaningfulness of these links.

> *It's good to know someone who has been through the experience.*
> *My best friend was adopted as a baby. It makes a difference.*
> *There was someone in my previous school who was adopted. That helped me.*

Regina (15) said that she felt guilty when she confided in her friend. Her foster carers insisted that they should be her sole confidantes.

> *My friend knows what I'm going through parent-wise. Her parents were too young to care for her. She doesn't fully understand why she was adopted. I do tell her things although my foster carers wouldn't approve if they knew. They would say that it was naughty.*

Three other children who did not know any other adopted or foster children said that they would have loved the opportunity to get to know someone else in their situation as it would prevent them from feeling 'different'.

Special friend

Twelve children identified a very special friend in their own age group who had helped them. Several said that they liked the fact that they had been able to tell this person about their fostering or adoption. Some teenagers said that they would require to trust their friend for several years before they would divulge any private details about their family history. Celia (9) had clear ideas about the qualities that she admired in her friend.

> *My friend understands me and listens. She knows I'm adopted. She stays around. She sticks up for me when I'm in pain.*

Three boys were aghast at the idea that they might confide in a school friend about their adoption, fostering or birth family circumstances. It was their opinion that their school-mates would 'laugh', 'ridicule' and 'take the mick'. Brendan (15) dismissed the suggestion that his classmates could offer him any support.

> *There would be absolutely no point in telling them. They wouldn't understand and they couldn't do anything.*

School

Life at school was an issue that children raised during their interview. It was often difficult for children to feel that they were understood within the context of school. Foster children especially felt 'different' and 'isolated'.

> *You feel that you're the only one in the world that's fostered. It makes me feel very different. I feel like there's a normal person and a disabled person. I feel like a disabled person.*

Children talked about being bullied at school, about other children's insensitive questions like, 'Why are you adopted?' and about panicking when they were asked to draw a family tree. Some children wanted the school to know that they were adopted while others were adamant that their adoption should remain a secret. Shane (15) recalled that when he was in primary school he used to lash out at other children when they asked him about adoption but now he has decided that it is best to be open about his status.

> *If I went to a job interview and I was asked I'd just say I was adopted at eight. My original parents were unable to look after me but I keep in contact with them. I've had a better education because I've been adopted. Adoption helps. In that way you tell the job person a bit about yourself and your character and they feel that they know you better.*

Paula (16) felt strongly that it should always be the child's choice whether the school was informed about adoption.

Chloe (17) had traumatic memories of transferring school as her different family placements disrupted. Each time she found her new classmates completely insensitive to her situation.

> *Kids would ask, 'Why are you going to a new school'? Children talk between themselves and can be nasty. They say, 'You've been nasty. You deserved it. You should be punished'. It's hard because the child has all that to listen to. The school should look into it.*

Recommendations

Children were asked whether they had any recommendations to make about new services. Many children made an overwhelming plea for their voice to be heard in all decision making about contact and for professional decisions to be fully explained to them. The fact that children should have the right to see their birth relatives if this was what they wanted was reiterated again and again. The following services were also requested:

- An independent advice centre run by experienced professionals. One child suggested Adopt Talk being available at this centre where there would be an opportunity to talk with other adopted children.
- A telephone help line offering a 'listening ear' and professional advice.
- An imaginative use of the internet through which adopted children could learn from the experiences of others.

Summary of Key Points

- ## Listening to children

  Children like to be able to express their views about all aspects of contact. This includes:
  - Which relatives they wish to see.
  - The contact venue.
  - The frequency of contact.
  - Contact activities.
  - Rules associated with contact.

  The contact plan should not be static. It is likely to require change at different phases of the placement. Professional time needs to be invested to listen to children's views again and again at different stages of the placement. Although a forum existed where this could happen for foster children there was not an equivalent system through which an adopted child's voice could continue to be heard.

- ## Purpose of contact

  A close emotional bond with the birth relative may exist, or this may be completely absent. Children have very different reasons for wanting contact with their birth relatives, such as:
  - To see for themselves that the birth relative is well.
  - To gain information as a means of understanding their origins and identity.
  - To place the blame for childhood abuse with the person who is culpable.

- ## Frequency of contact

  Children are likely to want much more contact with their birth relatives than their emotional resilience will allow, especially at the outset of their permanent placement. They will need help to understand why the level of contact that professionals recommend may not match their expectations.

- ## The emotional aspect

  Children are likely to have mixed and confused emotions about contact. It is important that they have an opportunity to express these complex emotions.

- **Confidentiality**

  The issue of confidentiality must be considered when choosing the contact venue. Otherwise the child may carry hidden fears about encountering previous abusers.

- **The impact on the child of negative and positive attitudes from adopters and foster carers towards birth relatives**

  Negative attitudes expressed verbally or non-verbally to the child by the adopters or foster carers towards the birth family affect the child adversely. On the other hand positive attitudes help the child manage the existence of their 'two families' more easily.

  Children benefited from seeing their 'two families' functioning well together at a social event. This seemed to give some continuity to the child's experiences of life, rather than fragmentation and disintegration.

- **Who should support the child during contact meetings?**

  Children who have recently joined their new family and who are beginning to make new parental attachments need their new parent at contact meetings with birth parents, in order to convey a clear message to them about who is the primary parent. This also enhances the child's feelings of security. On the other hand, teenagers who were more established in their placements often wanted to have a more neutral person to accompany them. It was difficult for a teenager to manage the emotional turmoil associated with having to relate simultaneously to 'two parents'.

- **Reviewing contact plans for adopted children**

  As children placed for adoption mature and become more established in placement, it is likely that contact plans will require to be adapted. It is therefore essential that a system for reviewing the original contact plan is established.

- **Relevant resources**

  Children and young people require ongoing access to independent advice about contact issues. An advice centre on contact could provide professional advice and mutual support from other adopted children.

  Some children like the idea of using internet services to learn about the experiences of other adopted children and young people.

CHAPTER 8

Sustaining, Supervising, Reviewing and Supporting Contact Plans

It was important that a clear contact plan was established at the beginning of the placement. It was also vital to ensure that an effective support structure was in place if contact arrangements were going to survive on a long-term basis. Most contact relationships did not evolve naturally and easily. They were usually intensely emotive experiences that tested the commitment of all parties. Adoptive parents and foster carers who had firsthand experience of personal trauma throughout their own childhood through the loss of significant family relationships had something special to offer: they were often determined to persevere despite relationship difficulties because they held a firm belief that contact with birth relatives was vital. Some birth relatives who drifted out of a child's life probably had no real sense of the importance that the child placed on retaining a live link with them.

Factors that Caused Contact with Adult Birth Relatives to Disintegrate

Thirty-five of the total sample of 106 children (33 per cent) were involved in contact plans that disintegrated after a period. This included 13 children who were in contact with adult birth relatives and 22 who were in contact with siblings. For some children this resulted in a complete loss of all ties with the birth family while for others it simply meant losing contact with one birth relative while sustaining a relationship with others.

Figure 17 illustrates the reasons for the collapse of contact relationships between children and their adult birth relatives, including birth parents, grandparents, aunts and uncles. In one case where the birth relatives were

Birth relative upsetting the child affecting the child's ability to settle	4
Birth relative rejecting child	4
Breakdown in relationship between birth relative and adoptive family	3
Child decided that contact was too stressful and requested termination	1
Birth relative's whereabouts became unknown	1

Total = 13 children.

Figure 17: Factors that caused contact with adult birth relatives to disintegrate

upsetting the child, social services had intervened to stop contact. In another two cases the adoptive parents made the decision to terminate contact and the birth parents were fighting legally for the right to see their children. The four children who experienced open rejection by their birth parents were devastated and yearned for the renewal of these relationships. One adopter could not conceal her emotion as she described her adopted son's anguish.

He'd welcome any crumbs of contact that the birth parents might offer him.

In the three cases where there had been a complete breakdown in the relationship between the adopters and the birth relatives it was noticeable that there was no intermediary who could have undertaken a placatory role. One 10-year-old girl who asked for contact with her birth mother to stop was clear about her reasons for this.

Thinking about what's happened is keeping me awake and I don't want to be reminded.

In the case where the birth mother's whereabouts were unknown, she had gone missing previously and been traced by social services. At the time of the study another search by social services was underway for her but after more than a year of lapsed contact hopes were fading of finding her. Prior to her disappearance she had told her son Scott (17) that she was suffering from a terminal illness but no one knew whether this was a true diagnosis. Scott's relationship with his birth mother was suspended in limbo and this was very unsettling for him.

Factors that Caused Contact with Siblings to Disintegrate

Figure 18 illustrates the reasons why sibling contact was not sustained. It was impossible to retain satisfactory relationships between siblings in separate placements when the adoptive families were in conflict. In one case where the adoptive parents had resorted to angry outbursts at each other, sibling contact relationships became equally volatile. When there was a change of social worker it was easy for contact arrangements to drift. When

Breakdown in relationship between different adopters or between adopters and birth relatives	6
Social worker leaving job	2
Birth parent blocking contact with sibling	4
Aftermath of contact was too distressing for the child	3
Fear of sibling who exhibited dominant or sexualised behaviour	3
Adoptive parents lacking commitment to contact plan	1
Child refused contact or one sibling rejected the other	2
Sibling's chaotic lifestyle	1

Total = 22 children.

Figure 18: Factors that caused contact with siblings to disintegrate

one sibling lived with birth parents the latter was in a very powerful position to impede sibling contact especially when contact plans had been established on a voluntary basis. Three children found the reality of contact with a sibling triggered too many sad memories while another three were simply overwhelmed by the level of control that another sibling was able to exert over them. One adoptive family who was left with sole responsibility for arranging sibling contact ignored the relevance of it and made no attempt to make the necessary practical arrangements. In situations where siblings were united in their wish for contact to terminate, everything was straightforward. In one case highlighted in Figure 18 (see page 118) where a sibling had refused contact this was not the case. Dean (12) had remained with his turbulent birth family while Miles (14) had been adopted. After several years in his affluent adoptive family Miles decided that he no longer shared his brother Dean's interests and values. When Dean was informed about his brother's decision his distress was visible to all around him and he required counselling in order to come to terms with his loss. Some older siblings who lived independently had such a turbulent lifestyle that it was almost impossible for them to make regular time and space for contact. In such circumstances the collapse of contact plans was inevitable.

The Role of an Intermediary in Sustaining Contact Plans

In ten out of the 26 adoption cases where contact collapsed the absence of an intermediary to resolve difficulties between the adopters and the birth family was a highly significant factor that contributed to the complete disintegration of contact. When tensions arose it was enormously difficult for the different parties to resolve their problems. Confusion surrounded questions like: Who holds ultimate responsibility for decision making? Whose needs should take priority when there are competing interests?

An Example of the Importance of an Intermediary in the Long Term Survival of a Difficult Contact Plan

James was five years old when he joined his adoptive family and he has now been there for more than nine years. Since placement he has retained contact twice annually with his birth mother and two younger sisters who lived with the birth mother. Although James's adoption was granted more than five years ago his single parent adopter continues to draw on the support of her social services social worker who arranges, supervises and supports the contact plan. When difficulties occur the adoptive mother uses her social worker as an intermediary to facilitate brokerage between all the parties. There has been a constant need to adjust the contact plan as the following complex situations have emerged.

The emotional component

The adoptive mother feels that nothing could have prepared her for the complex range of emotions that contact arouses. These include jealousy, anger, hatred and protectiveness.

The birth mother blocking contact between James and his special sibling

James has a very special bond with one of his younger sisters, Julia, for whom he had assumed a parenting role when they had lived together in the birth family. The birth mother is acutely jealous of this bond and wants all James's affection directed towards her. On occasions she has privately instructed Julia that she is to ignore James during contact meetings. James's level of anger has at times been uncontrollable.

Emotional pressure on child

The birth mother puts pressure on James to call her 'mum'. James feels 'torn in two directions' by this and tries to avoid the issue by not calling her anything.

Inappropriate conversations during contact meetings

The birth mother talks to James about her sexual exploits and Julia has also been sexually explicit towards him. Although James wants to see his birth family he is also frequently distressed by the reality of contact. The adoptive mother states that 'the birth mother is frequently messing James's head up'. The adoptive mother does have a network of friends and relatives who support her. Her mother always accompanies her to contact meetings. However, she does feel that her own family are too emotionally involved to be able to offer objective support and advice. The following factors have undoubtedly contributed to the long-term survival of contact in this case:

- The adoptive mother was offered a choice about whether she wished her social services social worker to continue to support her or to withdraw after adoption. She has wholeheartedly welcomed social services' continuing support.
- The adoptive mother describes social services as her 'hot line'. After a contact crisis she can offload her strong feelings to her social worker. The fact that she has a named social worker to turn to provides her with time to think through each situation and to act in a more balanced way.
- Her social worker enables her to think creatively about how to adapt the contact plan so that James's needs are always paramount. Plans are now underway for James to have a regular additional meeting with his sister Julia on his own. His birth mother is unhappy about this new arrangement but this new plan is about to be implemented with support from social services.

An Example of the Absence of an Intermediary and its Impact on the Collapse of Contact

Kevin (9), Lyn (8) and Rikki (6) are a sibling group who were placed for adoption. From the outset it was assumed that they would have contact with their grandfather and a half brother. Social services recommended that contact would occur at least twice a year but the details of how contact would work out were not specified. It was left to the discretion of the adopters to determine exactly how much contact was in the best interests of the children. An initial meeting between grandfather, his new wife and the prospective adopters occurred while the adoptive family was being assessed. It was highly successful and everyone returned home feeling quite euphoric. Grandfather made it clear that he liked the adopters.

Within six months both parties had met on three occasions either in the adopter's or birth relative's homes. This was three times the level of contact that had been recommended by social services. Then the tranquillity of the relationship was suddenly shattered when the grandfather's wife telephoned excitedly to suggest that it would be a good idea if they all went on holiday together. The adopters hesitated and politely asked for time to consider the holiday proposal. Two weeks later the grandfather's wife telephoned again to announce that the holiday had now been finalised and to request half payment. At this point the adopters stated clearly that they would not be going on holiday.

This crisis adversely affected relationships and led to a breakdown of all contact. These birth family relationships had been especially significant for Kevin who had a unique bond with his half brother. In this case both parties tended to treat the relationship as if it was as straightforward as any extended family relationship. With the benefit of hindsight the adoptive family felt that contact collapsed because of:

- The absence of an agreed framework and any type of written agreement.
- The lack of a third party to arbitrate.
- The overpowering influence of a dominant personality in the birth family.

The question of who should hold decision-making power in the event of a disagreement and who should arbitrate had never been raised either by social services or the voluntary agency that had recruited and prepared the adoptive family. Although contact has now been completely severed the adoptive family continue to carry anxiety about the fact that other abusive birth family members might be able to trace the children. The fact that the grandparents now have full knowledge about the whereabouts of the children has left this story unfinished.

Supervision

In 60 out of 106 cases formal supervision of contact meetings had been or continued to be provided either by a social services or voluntary agency social worker. In adoption cases it was rare for formal supervision to be provided beyond the legalisation of adoption. In fostering it was unusual for supervision to be available after the child attained 18 years.

Attitudes to supervision

Attitudes to social work supervision were predominantly positive. Only a very few people complained about it being invasive and intrusive. Generally it was perceived as easing tense relationships, and increasing feelings of safety. When a social worker was present contact plans were less likely to remain rigid and static as the social worker usually ensured that these plans were adjusted when difficulties accrued. Some social workers prepared a written report. Several families commented about the value of having an independent written assessment of what was happening. Most children and young people were positive about social work supervision too. Teenagers in particular liked the presence of an independent third party who did not have a high emotional investment in the process.

The absence of supervision

The absence of social work supervision was a serious issue in ten cases. In one case a very immature 16-year-old girl became the victim of sexual abuse by her older brother when social services relaxed supervision arrangements and gave her permission to visit her brother's flat on her own. In a very worrying case a birth father was able to use bribery, dominance and sexual innuendo with his six-year-old daughter while her foster carer provided supervision. She had alerted social services about the seriousness of this situation but she was informed that supervision could not be provided because of scarce resources. Following these encounters with her birth father this child's behaviour was deeply disturbed and at times almost hysterical. This placement disrupted after sixteen months.

Another adoptive father who provided supervision at a social services office was embarrassed as he witnessed the birth family's criminal tendencies.

They'd nick anything they could see in the social services' office: phones, mugs and cutlery. It was quite depressing.

The adoptive father made a conscious decision not to intervene in case it would jeopardise his tenuous relationship with the birth family. Instead he made a formal request to social services to supervise. This request was refused but he was told that he could call on a social worker in an adjacent office if problems escalated.

Tricia (12) is in foster care. Social services had agreed to provide formal supervision but the supervising social worker always failed to appear. This left the foster mother in a very difficult position as the birth family always tried to manipulate her into changing aspects of the contact plan. The foster mother lodged a complaint and a new social worker was allocated to provide supervision.

Suzy (16) raised the issue of wishing a social worker to be present at contact meetings at several fostering reviews. Her birth mother is an alcoholic who has secretly passed alcohol and drugs to Suzy. She worries about whether her birth mother will be drunk and how she should handle the situation if her birth mother's behaviour gets out of control. Her pleas to social services for supervision have been futile. Suzy feels that she is 'unprotected'.

In addition to the ten families who expressed concerns about the absence of social work supervision others talked about how rare it was for supervision to be available after the legalisation of adoption. Although some families liked the freedom of being independent of a social worker, others felt 'alone' and 'bereft' after adoption and would have liked to have had access to a flexible system through which they could obtain external supervision as and when they felt it was essential.

The absence of black social workers to supervise contact

A number of black families and social workers stated that they felt more comfortable when a black social worker was available to supervise contact. One black social worker employed by a voluntary agency described a placement of an eight-year-old black boy that had disrupted. She was convinced that if social services had allocated funding towards the provision of a black supervising social worker, this would have made a positive impact on the placement.

There are too few black social workers. A black family are not so relaxed with a white worker. There's no financial help from social services towards black social workers in voluntary agencies being able to be present at contact meetings.

The dilemmas associated with constant changes of social worker

Children were always seriously disadvantaged by constant changes of social worker. When a Care Order was granted for Terry (5) the Judge stressed the importance of contact between Terry and his older sister being handled sensitively. Terry's sister lived with grandparents and there was a danger that confidential information might be passed to Terry's abusive birth mother. The Judge stated that social services' monitoring would be central to the successful implementation of contact. He then went on to express confidence in the social worker. While the judge might have been right to admire the professional competence of one particular social worker, frequent changes of social worker became an enormous hindrance to good professional practice. A social worker from a voluntary adoption agency explained what actually happened.

There have been eight changes of social services' social worker in 18 months. There have been frustrations associated with not having a named person in social services to contact. Social services have struggled to provide a basic contact agreement. There have been huge delays. Social services had a contract to do Life Story work but it hasn't got done. The changes of social worker have been a huge source of frustration for the adopter.

Ed (11) has now been in placement for three years. Each time he has contact with his siblings a different social services' social worker provides supervision. The contact venue and the contact plan have remained unaltered despite the fact that the children have outgrown both. Recommendations for change made by Ed and his adopters after each contact meeting never get implemented because a new social worker appears on each occasion. The family feel disillusioned with social services. They want to continue with contact because Ed yearns to see his siblings but they feel as if the plan and the venue have become fossilised.

Supervision by adopters and foster carers

Some adopters and foster carers were highly skilled at working with difficult birth families. There were situations where a deliberate decision was made that social services should withdraw because the attitude of the birth family towards the statutory department was so negative. Chloe (16) retains contact twice annually with her birth mother. Her social worker feels that if social services had been supervising this contact arrangement it would have failed. She is convinced that it has succeeded because the adoptive mother has demonstrated exceptional skills when working with the birth family.

The adoptive mother's attitude has been key. Originally the birth family was very antagonistic to the adoption plan. The adoptive mother treated the birth family with respect and was able to coax them into trusting her. The adoptive family and the birth family have been able to adopt each other.

In contrast, there were other situations where an intolerable burden was placed on the adoptive family's shoulders by expecting them to take sole responsibility for supervision. Leon's (12) adoptive mother found that the strain associated with supervising all birth family contact brought both her and the placement close to breaking point. Prior to embarking on the contact plan she had not estimated how personally traumatised she would be by how birth family issues affected Leon.

It was difficult dealing with all the issues and at the same time trying to keep Leon safe. I felt exhausted. I usually felt either really angry or upset. I've had the disadvantage of not having anyone independent to witness how difficult contact had been. There should have been a third party at least up to the time of the Adoption Order.

Leon's adoptive mother feels as if she has not just adopted one very complex child but also his entire birth family. She described them all as childlike people who often made excessive demands on her waning energy.

Supervision by birth relatives

In two cases a birth relative had been nominated by social services to provide formal supervision. In one instance the supervisor was a grandmother whose role was to 'curtail birth mother's excesses' and in another it was an aunt who had been a professional foster carer. These supervision arrangements failed abysmally.

Brian was placed for adoption at 11 years. For the first six months social services provided supervision of contact between Brian and his birth father, birth mother, aunt, uncle and cousins. After six months, responsibility was transferred from social services to his aunt. This is how Brian's adopters assessed the quality of the aunt's supervision.

Supervision by the aunt failed and resulted in a near fatal mistake. When Brian was 14 years old he came home from contact saying that he wanted to see his lawyer. His birth father had bribed him to change his mind from adoption to fostering with the reward of a train set. Fostering would have been a violation of everything that we had worked for and the placement would have broken down. We'd have been sold down the river for a £70 train set and Brian would have been back in residential care.

A creative approach to supervision

There was one case that stood out from the others because an imaginative approach to supervision had been established.

Miles was eight when he joined his adoptive family while his brother Dean continued to live with the birth mother. Both boys had been brought up in a chaotic birth family but Miles had been the scapegoat. He was especially vulnerable because he resembled his estranged birth father. Incidents of non-accidental injury by the birth mother led to both boys being removed from the birth family on several occasions and ultimately to Miles being placed for adoption. Throughout their history Miles and Dean had had a special foster mother.

When the decision was made that the boys should be separated it was important to think carefully about how contact could be maintained between the boys. As Dean was still living with his birth family full consideration had to be given to the need to preserve confidentiality. It was especially important that the birth mother should not know about Miles' whereabouts.

A contact plan was devised that gave the special foster mother responsibility for supervising contact. The practicalities of the contact plan worked in the following way:

- The birth mother contacted the foster carer.
- The foster carer rang the adopters.
- The foster carer collected Dean from his birth family.
- The contact meeting occurred in a neutral venue such as a family restaurant or a park.
- The foster carer who was very experienced in working with difficult children supervised the contact meeting.

This contact arrangement survived many difficulties and lasted for five years with both boys seeing each other twice annually. The social services' social worker described the factors that she felt contributed towards the success of this contact plan.

- An experienced foster carer who was committed to giving up two Saturdays annually to undertake supervision.
- A neutral venue.
- A social worker who had worked with the birth family over many years and knew both boys.
- Good communication between the adopters and the foster carer.
- The adopters' concerns about confidentiality were put at ease by the foster carer.
- Vigilant supervision. When Dean asked Miles, 'Where do you live?' the foster carer knew how to step in discreetly.

As the social worker reflected on this case she commented:

The foster mother's supervision was the key to contact working. It avoided the formality of a social worker and it prevented confidentiality problems because the foster carer was tuned in to the issues.

Reviewing of Contact Plans

Children and young people who were in foster care had the opportunity of having their contact plans evaluated regularly through the formal review system. This enabled the contact plan to be adjusted if necessary.

In adoption there was no forum where contact plans could be regularly reviewed. When adoptive families were working closely with their social worker informal discussions about the need for change did occur and appropriate changes were implemented. Adoptive families who preferred to function independently were at a disadvantage when tensions occurred between the different parties involved in contact or when children outgrew the original contact plan. In these circumstances neither party was sure who held the power to instigate change. It was easy for a contact plan to reach stalemate and for adults to develop an entrenched position. There was a constant danger that the principle of a child's best interests being paramount could be forgotten while adult wrangles predominated.

Support

Who is your greatest source of support in relation to contact issues?

Voluntary agency	Social services	Partner	Extended family	Friend	Nobody
40	15	13	12	10	8
Self	Birth relative	Other adopter or foster carer	The child in placement	Psychotherapist	School
7	5	5	5	1	1

Some families nominated more than one source as their greatest support.

Figure 19: Who is your greatest source of support in relation to contact issues? The verdict of adopters and foster carers

Figure 19 illustrates who the adoptive parents and foster carers considered to be their greatest source of support in relation to contact difficulties. A recurring theme was that families were looking for professional support. Contact was perceived as a complex issue that was often not readily understood within their network of family and friends.

When I had problems I always turned to the voluntary agency and social services. They're professional. That's the kind of service that you need. It's the same idea as turning to a doctor with a medical problem.

Support through the voluntary agency

The majority of families were positive about the help derived through the voluntary adoption agency. Complimentary phrases were used like; 'They were always there for us'; 'They were an excellent go between'; 'The social worker was really skilled'; 'They were able to talk at the child's level'. However, there was a tendency to turn more frequently to social services rather than the voluntary agency when difficulties with contact occurred and only to approach the voluntary agency when they reached an impasse with social services. This was because responsibility for working with the birth family usually rested with social services and the resolution of difficulties with the birth family therefore usually lay outside the domain of the voluntary agency. Some families did use their voluntary agency social worker to ventilate their strong emotions about what was happening. In a number of difficult contact relationships a social worker from the voluntary agency undertook an independent assessment of the impact on the child of the contact relationship and then made a recommendation about continuing or severing contact.

Support through social services

There were some examples of good partnerships between adopters or foster carers and social services. This was especially true when the same social worker had been in post on a long-term basis and had known the child over many years. However, there were also negative examples of very impoverished relationships that left families feeling totally exasperated. Most families had gained the impression during their preparation and assessment that the issue of contact was a high priority for social services departments. They therefore assumed that supporting contact plans would be an equal priority for all social services departments. Some were devastated when they discovered that this high quality service did not exist. Frustration was expressed about the anonymity of the service and the slow and sometimes obstructive response that they received to their queries. This was how one adoptive family described their experience of seeking support.

> During our preparation, contact was the buzz word. The importance of it was stressed by social services over and over again. Initially contact with the birth mother was driven by social services. Our social worker was a lovely person and we felt supported. She was like a friend.
>
> I naïvely assumed that if a problem arose after adoption that I'd ring social services and they would sort it out. We discovered that after adoption social services don't really want to know. Each time we have to arrange contact the birth mother is living somewhere different. I've had to force social services to find her. It's been a battle. Trying to organise the visits has been a nightmare. Each time we telephone social services it's someone different dealing with it. I'd sum it up by saying social services are OK if you can kick them up the a***.

Another family reached a crisis point with their adopted teenager and urgently needed to help him fill in the blanks in his background history.

> We went on holiday. Chris (13) was very intense. Things were coming up in a school project about the family and he needed to know things about his birth mother. He wanted to know why he had asthma. Was it because his birth mother smoked? What time was he born? How much did he weigh as a baby?
>
> I rang social services. They gave me the impression, 'What on earth are you ringing us for?' There was no one that could talk to him about the past. Social services were obstructive.

I was angry. They were prepared to give us an Adoption Allowance but they weren't prepared to do any of the emotional stuff. I kept wondering, 'Where's this after-support that they talk about?'

These families and others who were disappointed with the quality of support service that they received echoed a similar plea.

We need a named person in social services who will take responsibility for contact issues.

Partnership between voluntary and statutory agencies

In some cases partnerships between statutory and voluntary agencies worked smoothly. Some families were equally enthusiastic about the quality of service that they received from both sources. Phrases from families like, 'It's been straightforward' and 'We've been so lucky' indicated how positive relationships between statutory and voluntary agencies impacted on them.

Many of the difficulties that voluntary agency staff described in working with social services seemed to originate from constant changes of social services staff. Voluntary agency staff talked about their immense frustration when contact agreements were not drafted, children's reviews were delayed, children's background histories were not compiled and children's Life Story work was forgotten.

The project leader of one voluntary agency described how she had learned after a number of difficult experiences of failed partnerships with social services that it was imperative to ensure that all service agreements with social services addressed exactly who would provide long term support in relation to contact.

Part of our contract with social services states that they must provide a named post holder who will be responsible after adoption for contact. This has proved to be a useful arrangement. We developed this after learning the hard way. In one case we ended up having to go out and search for the birth mother.

Support after adoption

There was a plea from families who had adopted through both voluntary and statutory agencies for a much greater level of post-adoption support. Some described how their difficulties increased rather than decreased as the placement elongated.

You need post-adoption support. There's not enough of that. The behaviour of Elaine (8) after contact has been more challenging than we would have expected. It's been a steep learning curve. Our first year was less awful. The second and third years were more difficult.

Some families disliked the 'open door' post-adoption service because it placed the onus on their shoulders to cry for help. They recommended a more pro-active service.

We got a lot of help in the first eighteen months. Once the adoption was through we got little post-adoption support. We had to handle it ourselves. My feelings were knocked and bruised by what was happening through contact. It was stressful and difficult. No one bothered about us. There was no nursing for us. There were no positive strokes. That upset me. Post-adoption support needs to be pro-active, not reactive.

Support through other adopters and foster carers

It was noticeable and rather surprising to discover how little families drew on the support of other adopters and foster carers. This type of informal support network was rarely set up for adopters by the placing agency. One adoptive family was formally linked with a support foster carer whom they described as a 'brick'. A few families had close friends who happened to have adoption or fostering experience. However, these positive links were rare. Families presented a number of reasons for rejecting the potential usefulness of this source of support:

- Many adoptive families were convinced that the majority of adopters disapproved of the concept of contact. This impression had usually arisen through listening to debates and arguments about contact during preparation groups. Many felt that their positive attitude towards contact was unique. It was therefore pointless to look to other adopters for advice and support.
- Contact issues were perceived as very complex because birth families often had to cope with a host of difficulties, and professional solutions were therefore imperative.
- Many adopters felt that they would be betraying their child's trust if they talked openly about background factors and birth family dilemmas. The following comment from one adoptive mother typified sentiments expressed by others.

What's happening between our adopted children and their birth mother isn't information that we'd share easily. It's hard to find anyone that we'd trust enough.

Adopters' support groups were unpopular because they often focussed on negative experiences.

The self help group was so negative. It made us depressed. It reminded us of the problems. When they talked about Attachment Disorder it made me nervous. We needed positive input during the times that we felt we couldn't cope. We needed to feel that there was hope.

There were practical problems associated with attending adopters groups too. The level of difficulty that most children presented was high. At the end of a stressful day there was not enough time and energy available to attend a group meeting where discussions often seemed to be repetitive rather than providing positive and practical strategies.

Some adopters suggested that they would prefer to watch videos describing the real experiences of other families. A number mentioned that they would like to gain knowledge through the internet rather than using any type of telephone link with other foster carers or adopters.

Financial support underpinning contact plans

The greatest difficulties surrounding financial support underpinning contact plans, concerned adopters. Some adopters were eligible for an Adoption Allowance. Occasionally this allowance was enhanced to ensure that travel and subsistence costs for contact meetings were included. Birth relative's travel and subsistence costs were sometimes paid by social services but it was rare for an equivalent arrangement to exist for adopters. A number of adopters were not only paying their own and their children's costs but they also paid for meals and entertainment for the birth relatives. Some adopters admitted that the degree of contact that was feasible was dictated by financial considerations rather than by what was in the best interests of the child.

Whether any financial support was available for any aspect of the contact arrangement depended on which geographical area an adoptive family lived in and on which social services department was involved. Many adopters resented the fact that they were expected to finance contact meetings without any acknowledgement from social services about the difficulties that this entailed.

> We pay over £100 on our tickets alone. There's absolutely no reimbursement. If it was 50/50 it wouldn't be so expensive. It's difficult.

In contrast, foster carers were usually able to get their travel and subsistence costs paid on a regular basis in conjunction with their monthly fostering allowance.

Support through psychotherapy

There were different stages in the placement when children needed access to psychotherapeutic services because they were struggling to come to terms with trauma that had occurred within their birth family. Strong feelings were triggered for some children by the reality of contact and for others by the absence of contact. Some children were able to make positive use of psychotherapeutic services while others found it too difficult to trust anyone however skilled they might be. One adopter who described psycho-therapeutic services as beneficial for herself readily admitted that it had not worked for her nine-year-old adopted son.

> Scott (9) set his face against any intervention and he never took his head out of his anorak.

Another adopter commented:

John (9) has a very poor ego and he didn't want to give anything away that would give the therapist a bad opinion of him. It takes him a long time to free up. After a year of weekly therapy he simply chose what it was safe to talk about.

Some children and young people who were interviewed for the research study presented a very positive view of therapy. They felt that therapy had helped them to discuss their problems more openly. One teenager felt that a psychotherapeutic service should have been made available to her as soon as she was removed from her birth family despite the fact that she was very young.

I was 12 years old when I had my first talk with a psychotherapist. I should have been allowed to talk with the psychotherapist at 5 years when I was first taken away from my family. By the time I was 12 I was trying to cope on my own. It was too late to tell me how to handle my feelings. If I'd had help earlier I'd have been able to talk more confidently.

In some instances psychotherapy was recommended but the child had to join a long waiting list at a critical juncture in their lives due to scarce psychotherapeutic resources.

Some children needed therapy many years after the finalisation of adoption. Often adopters paid privately for this service themselves. An example of this is an adoptive family with three siblings, Vicky (9) Celia (11) and Rachel (12). They had been parted abruptly from their birth mother with no opportunity to say goodbye when they were all of pre-school age. At the time of the research study they were just beginning a series of psycho-therapeutic sessions. It was envisaged that contact with the birth mother might be instigated for these teenagers with the psychotherapist acting as intermediary.

The Need for a Wider Education

There were many examples in the study of different people showing a complete lack of understanding about why a child might want to retain contact with members of their birth family. It was disconcerting for Sean (9) when his grandfather suggested bluntly, 'Just forget about these people from your past'.

There were also instances of hospital staff being bewildered as birth parents and adoptive parents sat by the bedside of an adopted child who was dying. Doctors and nurses were not quite sure which set of parents to consult and whose wishes should take priority. Some teachers reprimanded adopted children for fabricating the number of brothers and sisters that they had. In fact the children were proudly adding the numbers in their adoptive and birth family together.

The subject of adoption and contact is relatively new. It is only recently that adoptive parents and professionals have started to wrestle with the complexities involved. Research that highlights some of the positive influences of a more open style of adoption is a recent phenomenon. The study indicates that a much wider education is required if children are going to benefit from a sensitive response from key people around them. This type of education needs to include the adopters extended family, medical staff, teachers and the legal profession.

Summary of Key Points

- ### The need for an intermediary

  Contact relationships were often very intricate. The potential for conflict between the different parties was high. The availability of an intermediary to intervene when difficulties occurred had a positive impact on the continuation of contact.

- ### Supervision

  There is a need to think creatively about who might provide formal supervision for contact. Would it be possible to set up a pilot scheme that involved recruiting and training a range of people with different skills to undertake this important role? Some families recommended providing training for a range of professionals such as teachers and clergy. This type of scheme could also include people from minority ethnic backgrounds.

- ### Reviewing contact plans

  A system exists for reviewing all aspects of fostering placements including contact plans. Such a system does not exist for children who are legally adopted. As adoption placements elongated children's contact needs changed. Many adoptive families requested the existence of a review system where contact plans could be regularly evaluated and adapted to meet changing need.

- ### The critical nature of professional support

  Families were unanimous about the critical importance of a professional support service underpinning contact arrangements. This was the preferred option rather than any type of self-help through other adopters or foster carers.

- ### Post adoption support

  The fact that contact plans survived up until adoption did not necessarily mean that these plans would automatically continue to run smoothly. Support after adoption in relation to contact issues was often noticeably absent leaving some families feeling very isolated. Some contact plans that were very important to children disintegrated after adoption because there was not an adequate professional support structure underpinning the plan. Adopted and foster children were often very immature and needed support long after they had reached the age of 18 years. Black and Asian families often felt more comfortable if their social worker's ethnic background was similar to their own. Families made a request for a proactive rather than a reactive post-adoption service.

- **Financial support underpinning contact in adoption placements**

  Adoption with contact has resource implications. Contact planning must be underpinned by an appropriate social services' financial budget. There was often an unspoken agenda about the financial aspect of contact and a silent expectation that adopters would be prepared to meet contact costs associated with travel, subsistence and entertainment. Adopters resented this and there were occasions when an inadequate contact plan was implemented because the adoptive family's finances were limited.

- **Voluntary and statutory agencies working together**

  In order to overcome the difficulties associated with frequent changes of social services staff, voluntary agencies found it helpful to have a service agreement whereby a named post holder in social services agrees to carry responsibility for post adoption contact issues.

- **Psychotherapeutic services**

  Psychotherapeutic services are likely to continue to be required for some children long after adoption. Due to the complex nature of the children currently requiring adoption such a service needs to be an integral part of any post-adoption service.

- **Access to information and debate about adoption with contact**

  There is a need for more information about contact issues, and for the debate to extend beyond the social work profession, if children's needs are to be understood and responded to in a sensitive manner by a range of professional and lay people with whom the child is likely to interact on a day-to-day basis. Children's needs would be served more effectively if those people closest to them had a wider knowledge about the rationale underpinning contact, and greater opportunities to engage in a fuller debate about this important subject.

CHAPTER 9

Summary, Conclusions and Recommendations

General Conclusions

The children who feature in this study were placed in permanent fostering and adoptive families because of extremely neglectful or abusive experiences within their birth families. Some children had been grossly abused within a familial paedophile network. Despite the level of abuse most children were eager to retain contact with their birth relatives. However, the reality of face-to-face contact often provoked painful dormant feelings. Children's feelings towards their birth relatives were sometimes very changeable, often immensely complex and could at times be quite overwhelming. Retaining contact was therefore not an easy experience for the child, the birth relatives or the permanent foster and adoptive family.

An overview of the effect on children of contact with adult birth relatives

The following picture is based on a collation of the perceptions of foster carers, adopters, social workers, children and young people:

- For the majority of children who had contact with adult birth relatives there were both positive and negative effects. Contact with birth parents could be especially difficult leaving some children sad, disillusioned, with divided loyalties, and sometimes embittered by past memories. Despite this, children were resolute in their wish to see their birth relatives.
- The most vulnerable child was the one who had undertaken a quasi-parental role with a birth relative during early childhood. This child usually demonstrated intense feelings about contact and seemed unable to relinquish an inappropriate sense of responsibility towards the birth relative whom they had parented.
- Children whose birth parents refused to see them conveyed the impression that this was much more devastating than living with the reality of an impoverished contact relationship.
- In five cases contact with birth parents was perceived as a central issue that led to placement disruption.
- In a further ten cases contact with birth parents was perceived either by adopters, foster carers or social workers as a factor that seriously undermined the stability of the placement, bringing some 'to the brink of disruption'. In some situations it was not contact itself that was causing

difficulties but excessive levels of contact that did not allow sufficient recovery time between one contact meeting and the next for the distraught child and the overwrought adoptive family.

An overview of the effect on children of contact with siblings

- Sibling contact was a predominantly positive experience for the majority of children. When it did create serious difficulties for a minority of children it was usually terminated very promptly. It was therefore not an issue that seriously affected the stability of the placement or contributed directly towards the placement disrupting.
- The termination of a significant sibling relationship was deeply traumatic for a small number of children.

Frequency of contact (adult birth relatives)

- Professional expectations about the degree of contact between foster and adoptive children and adult birth relatives that could be tolerated in permanent placements were often unrealistically high. This was especially true in relation to fostering placements where the frequency of contact was sometimes planned as often as fortnightly or monthly. However, in practice contact meetings often reduced in frequency as erratic birth parents just could not manage to keep these frequent appointments.
- In adoption placements, when contact with birth parents was established at a level greater than four times annually, the frequency usually had to be reduced to make it more viable.

Frequency of contact (siblings)

- Sibling contact was different to contact with adult birth relatives because it did not produce the same emotional aftermath and consequently had the potential to be sustained at a higher level than four times annually. However, it was vital that the frequency was practically manageable for all the parties involved.
- Practical barriers that adversely affected the amount of contact that could occur between siblings were:
  - Geographical distance between siblings.
  - The fact that there was rarely any type of financial framework supporting the contact arrangement.
  - Poor relationships between the carers involved.

Ascertaining children's wishes and feelings

A central tenet of all good social work practice is the importance of ascertaining children's wishes and feelings before making crucial childcare decisions. Just over one-third of the children and young people who were interviewed for this study felt that they had been adequately consulted by social workers about contact. However, some children felt cheated because decisions about contact had been made without any reference to their wishes. In other situations children felt aggrieved because they were not consulted about all aspects of the contact plan. It was clear that children did not just want to be asked once for their opinion but they wanted opportunities for ongoing dialogue as they matured and their feelings about contact were liable to change. Foster children had the advantage of being able to express whether their views had changed at regular childcare reviews. In contrast adopted children did not have a forum where their voice could be heard. When they confided in their adopters, the latter felt and were frequently powerless to effect change unless social services acted on their behalf. Many expressed disappointment and disillusionment about the low priority that social services placed on their requests. Frequent changes in social services' personnel and the absence of a named social worker or key post holder resulted in families often finding that the service provided was frustratingly slow and impersonal.

Explaining childcare decisions to children

Childcare decisions need to be explained fully to children at a level that they can comprehend. The rationale underpinning decisions to split siblings may be complex. How do children perceive reasons for placing their sibling in a separate family, such as the risk of sexual activity occurring between siblings, dominance by one sibling over another, or the excessive emotional needs of one child detracting from the other? Another problem is that children are likely to want a much higher level of contact than their emotional resilience will allow. Professional time needs to be invested with children exploring these issues in a child-focussed way. If this groundwork is not completed the feelings emanating from children's private resentments and misunderstandings will impinge on contact relationships.

Preparation for adopters and foster carers

Most families felt positively about the preparation for contact that social workers offered them during their assessment period. Social workers were often zealous about the concept of contact and succeeded in transforming the attitudes of some sceptical families. Some families from minority ethnic and religious backgrounds found it easier to relate to the concept of contact if it was explained within the framework of their cultural beliefs. Some new adopters felt overawed by the amount of material that they were required to absorb during their preparation and assessment and recommended that detailed discussions about contact issues should be deferred until after their application had been approved by the adoption panel. Prospective adopters who had previously fostered had the advantage of previous experience of working with birth relatives.

Ongoing training after placement was also recommended. Some preferred the idea of distance learning and education through the internet because of the practical difficulties associated with attending training events when all their energy was being absorbed by the demands of a dysfunctional child.

Assessment of risk

A critical question in this study is: how do professionals ensure that contact plans are implemented in such a way as to ensure that children are safeguarded from further risk of abuse? It was tempting to want to retain spontaneity and flexibility in contact relationships at the expense of safety. There were serious dangers associated with opening connections between children and their abusive birth relatives too widely while disregarding vital aspects such as confidentiality and anonymity. The study indicates that detailed written contact agreements are essential and that a contact plan needs to have firm boundaries about who? what? when? where? and how? in order to have adequate safeguards in place.

When considering which contact venue to use it is important to undertake an analysis of the long-term risks associated with opening up sensitive connections. The most convenient venue for contact at the outset of the placement may be the adoptive home but this immediately places the child's anonymity under threat. It is especially important to trace the links that may exist between the birth family member involved in contact and the wider abusive birth family network. Due to the dysfunctional nature of many of the birth families involved in this study it was often difficult to assess how family relationships would evolve. Many had an erratic quality about them. Some relationships that were potentially damaging to the child did not seem at first glance to pose a threat because they had been severed in acrimonious circumstances. However, this study is a reminder of how easily unsavoury relationships in abusive families could be rekindled.

Contact between siblings after disruption

When siblings were placed together and one placement disrupted professionals often wanted to rush headlong into the retention of a contact relationship between the siblings. There was an expectation that the adopters who had just experienced disruption would be an active part of this contact arrangement. Although these links were probably vital for the children the reality was that the adopters were still living through a kind of bereavement as they emerged from the trauma of disruption. Consequently they were unable to respond positively. In some instances they openly rejected the child. In others they made inappropriate conditional promises to the child about returning to live with them. It was clear that the adopters who had experienced the trauma of disruption needed time to work through critical stages of grief before they could manage to participate in contact plans in a manner that reflected the child's best interests.

Support

There were serious gaps in the provision of support to families in relation to the outworking of contact plans. This was especially true for adopters as the placement elongated beyond the stage of legalised adoption. Financial support was erratic for adopters; there was no system for monitoring the effectiveness of contact plans; it was difficult for families to draw on the support of a third party who could provide brokerage when contact plans became too fraught for the different parties to be able to achieve an easy resolution. Only the most persistent adopters succeeded in getting their requests met when they asked social services to facilitate changes in an existing contact plan, or to trace birth relatives who had opted out of contact plans, or to respond to children's pleas to see additional birth relatives. Formal supervision arrangements for vulnerable adopted and fostered teenagers were sometimes terminated because of scarce resources even though this left the immature young person open to further risk of abuse. Lack of support resulted in some potentially positive contact relationships disintegrating. The study indicates that the area of support for contact plans needs to be radically reconsidered if potentially useful contact relationships are going to survive on a long-term basis.

Specific Recommendations

Contact planning

- Consult the child. Children are liable to want unrealistically high levels of contact. Time needs to be invested explaining to the child why this may not be viable.
- Consider potential barriers to contact working effectively. Are any of the parties involved likely to impede contact? Are there ways of overcoming and minimising these impediments?
- Analyse the risks for the child of confidentiality and anonymity being jeopardised. Are there direct and indirect links between the person retaining contact and the child's previous abusers? Even if the immediate risks may seem minimal are there long-term risks?
- It is vital that children understand professional decisions about splitting them from a sibling. If this groundwork is not thoroughly addressed, unresolved issues are likely to adversely affect sibling contact.
- Which adults should accompany the child to early contact meetings? Excluding prospective adopters from attending initial contact meetings

with birth parents at a stage when the child is beginning to make crucial new family attachments may be distressing for an insecure child and convey the wrong message to the child about who is the primary parent.

- Sibling contact is more likely to be sustainable between children placed in different adoptive families when the adopters are compatible in terms of class, values and aspirations. Wide differences and tensions between adopters are liable to drive a wedge between siblings.
- Consider whether the timing and degree of contact takes account of the child's need to attach to a new family and the adopter's need to claim the child. If the birth relatives are in agreement to the placement an early contact meeting may be very reassuring to the child. If the birth relatives are opposed to the placement the child should be given several months to enhance feelings of security in the placement without having to face the tensions associated with contact.

Preparing foster and adopted children for contact

- Children need careful preparation for contact and need to be reassured that adults will step in to protect them if difficulties ensue. Some children may benefit from role-playing the contact meeting, prior to embarking on it. Children who are unable to tolerate changes in their routine may need every minute detail of the contact event explained in advance to them or written down in simple child-friendly language.
- Children need to be clear about the names that they will use for all the different parties involved in contact meetings. The terms 'mum' and 'dad' may be especially contentious. Ground rules need to be established about what is permissible during contact meetings. Social workers need to ensure that all parties are aware of the significance of such sensitive issues in advance of contact meetings and that they are managed in a way that reflects the best interests of children.

Preparation and assessment

- Prospective adopters' negative attitudes to contact can be transformed through training and particularly through opportunities to think about birth family contact from the child's perspective.
- An important area to address when assessing the suitability of prospective adopters and foster carers is how personal childhood experiences of broken family relationships are liable to impinge on their attitudes to contact. A level of self-awareness will prevent adopters and foster carers from allowing their own experiences to eclipse the uniqueness of each child's situation.
- Behaviour difficulties such as dominance or sexual exploitation of one sibling over the other, which may have played a part in the decision to

split siblings, are liable to resurface during contact meetings. Preparation should be made for this in order to safeguard the interests of children.

- Contact issues do not just need to be addressed during the assessment and preparation period. Some families felt overwhelmed by the amount of new material that they were required to absorb at this juncture. Contact needs to continue to be an issue on the agenda for post placement training. Training workshops, distance learning packages and education through the internet were all recommended.

Preparation of birth relatives for contact

- Although birth relatives were not interviewed for this study, it is clear from the research data that birth relatives often lacked basic preparation for contact meetings. It is essential that social workers invest time with birth relatives, enabling them to think in advance of contact meetings about the impact of their words and behaviour on the lives of vulnerable children.

Frequency of contact

- The degree of contact needs to be manageable for all parties.
- Contact with siblings could be sustained at a much higher level than contact with birth parents because it usually did not evoke such highly emotive feelings. Children's attitudes to sibling contact often underwent change as their placement elongated. They frequently wanted less rather than more sibling contact as their relationships with their new family became more established and secure. The practicalities of wide geographical distance between carers, lack of financial support, and poor relationships between carers impeded sibling contact.
- When contact between children placed in adoptive families and their birth parents was established at more than four times annually it usually had to be reduced in order for it to be sustainable on a long term basis. It was rare for children to want to reduce their level of contact with their birth parents as their placement elongated.
- Contact between adopted or foster children and their birth parents that was set at a low level of once annually produced some particular problems. It was difficult for any degree of continuity to be maintained from one contact meeeting to the next and consequently children were liable to fantasise about their birth parents. It was often impossible to assess in advance exactly what changes might have occurred in the birth parents' situation during the intervening year. Annual contact therefore became a major unusual event for the child that could evoke high levels of anxiety.

Written contact agreements

- Written contact agreements are essential. They need to be specific with clear rules and boundaries around the plan.
- Children should be involved in the development of contact agreements which should be prepared in a child-friendly manner.
- A written contact agreement should be set in place at the outset of the placement. It will require refinement as the placement progresses.
- A written contact agreement should outline a framework for resolving any differences that might arise. The question of who holds decision-making power in the event of disagreement needs to be clarified.

The question of venue

- Good quality contact venues are a scarce resource. Most families and children wanted a neutral venue that was separate from a social services' office.
- The feasibility of suitable neutral venues being established in different geographical locations through a partnership between social services and voluntary agencies is one way of taking this issue forward. These venues need to be activity based, comfortable, private, secure and fun environments that can be open at flexible hours.
- Although children often liked the idea of their sibling visiting them in their adoptive family, it is important to consider the issue of confidentiality before agreeing to this. Do any of the siblings have direct or indirect links to any members of the abusive family network? Is this likely to raise a significant child protection risk either now or in the future?
- It is important to review the suitability of the venue. It needs to reflect the age and stage of development of the child. Children are likely to outgrow certain venues.

Supervision

- Children who have experienced an abusive childhood are likely to mature slowly. Contact supervision needs to take account of this vulnerability and in some cases requires to extend beyond the time when adoption is legalised and beyond 18 years for children in foster care. The early termination of supervision arrangements for some children in this study raised some serious child protection issues.
- In order to counteract the lack of social services personnel available to undertake supervision a creative scheme could be established whereby people with a range of different backgrounds and skills could be trained to undertake the task of supervision. Including people from different cultural backgrounds in this scheme would enable black children and their families to be linked with a supervisor from a similar minority ethnic background.

Mediation

- It is essential that a third party is available to provide brokerage and to facilitate contact relationships. Some families may not require this service but it should be accessible.
- Teenagers felt torn when an adoptive parent accompanied them to face-to-face contact meetings with their birth parents. They would have preferred a neutral person to accompany them but there was no readily identifiable scheme to turn to for this service.

Financial support

- Contact plans need to be underpinned by an adequate financial budget. Ad hoc financial arrangements hindered the outworking of some contact plans.

Review system for contact in adoption

- The absence of a system for reviewing contact plans in adoption cases was a disadvantage. Consequently, it was difficult for adopters to alter a contact plan even when it was clear that it was no longer in the child's best interests. There was a danger that contact plans became 'frozen' at a particular phase in the child's development.

Post adoption service

- A post-adoption service is essential if contact plans are going to be sustained in the long term.
- Some families recommended that this service should be separate from social services' statutory work or that social services should contract with the private sector to run this service.
- Essential components of this post-adoption service would be:
  - A professional support service rather than a service run by other adopters.
  - A pro-active rather than a reactive service providing emotional support and the availability of independent experienced personnel to accompany teenagers and young people to contact meetings if and when this was required.
  - A named key worker responsible for contact issues.
  - A larger number of black social workers to support contact arrangements for children from minority ethnic backgrounds.
  - An independent advice centre providing either face-to-face or telephone counselling to all parties involved in contact relationships.
  - Internet access providing networking between adoptive families.

The Way Forward: Some Personal Reflections

At the conclusion of this study it seems appropriate to permit a 12-year-old girl to have the final say:

Please tell social workers to let us see our birth relatives for the simple reason that they are our real relations.

This girl's opinion echoes the sentiments expressed by many children and young people who participated in this study. Despite the difficulties inherent in contact relationships, the majority of children were very eager for contact to happen. Contact with birth relatives is therefore likely to continue to be an important aspect of adoption and fostering practice throughout the 21st century.

However, the study illustrates that professionals need to proceed carefully and cautiously as they initiate and implement contact plans. This is especially true when children have emerged from difficult and complex family backgrounds. Safeguards need to be established in every contact plan to protect the short term and long term welfare of children. Contact arrangements should never be vague with responsibility for their outworking left solely in the hands of the parties directly involved. Instead, clear and detailed contact plans need to be fully negotiated between professionals and all the parties concerned. Written contact agreements enhance clarity and prevent misunderstandings. At the same time it is a mistake for contact plans to remain static. Instead, they need to keep pace with the changing needs of children. In this study, the absence of a formal system for reviewing contact plans in adoption was a serious gap in professional practice and resulted in some contact arrangements stagnating.

Social worker's zeal for the theoretical concept of contact was very obvious to foster carers and adopters during their assessment and preparation period. This professional enthusiasm needs to extend into the post placement period and result in a very practical long-term support service, available to all parties, and extending beyond the stage of legalised adoption. It is vital that none of the parties involved in contact are left isolated and bereft of someone neutral to whom they can turn for advice, consultation or arbitration when tensions occur. Sometimes a foster or adopted young person may simply need a listening ear; at other times they may need someone neutral who understands the complexity inherent in a contact relationship to accompany them on a sensitive encounter with a birth relative. If these safeguards are not in place, potentially useful contact relationships are likely to flounder and disintegrate. When these measures are established some of the most vulnerable children in our society can be helped to make sense of the trauma that they have suffered in their birth family, understand the conflicting emotions associated with their past, feel reassured through face-to-face contact about the welfare of their birth relatives, begin to make sense of their identity and move forward into the future with a sense of hope and optimism.

References

Argent, H. (1995) *See You Soon: Contact with Children Looked After by Local Authorities.* BAAF.

BAAF (1999) *Contact in Permanent Placement: Guidance for local authorities in England, Wales and Scotland.* BAAF.

Beckett, S. (1993) *A Study of Social Work Planning and Decision-making in Respect of Sibling Groups who were Accommodated or Looked After.* University of Birmingham dissertation and in Mullender, A. (Ed.) *We are Family: Sibling Relationships in Placement and Beyond.* BAAF.

Beckett. S. (1999) Fostering Siblings Together. In Wheal, A. (Ed.) *The RHP Companion to Foster Care.* Russell House Publishing.

Berry, M. (1991) The Effects of Open Adoption on Biological and Adoptive Parents and the Children: The Arguments and The Evidence. *Child Welfare.* 70(6).

Berry, M. (1993) Adoptive Parents' Perceptions of and Comfort with Open Adoption. *Child Welfare.* 72 (3).

Bilson, A. and Barker, R. (1993) Siblings of Children in Care or Accommodation: A Neglected Area of Practice. *Practice.* 6:4.

Bowlby, J. (1951) *Maternal Care and Mental Health.* World Health Organisation, Geneva.

Bowlby, J. (1986) The Making and Breaking of Affectional Bonds. In *Working with Children.* BAAF.

Dance, C., Cullen, D. and Collier, F. (1997) *Focus on Adoption; A Snapshot of Adoption Patterns in England, 1995.* BAAF.

Department of Health (1991) *Patterns and Outcomes in Child Placement.* HMSO.

Fitsell, A. (1992) *Genetic Sexual Attraction: Sexual Attraction Following Reunion.* London, Post Adoption Centre.

Fratter, J. (1996) *Adoption with Contact: Implications for Policy and Practice.* London, BAAF.

Fratter, J., Rowe, J., Sapsford, D. and Thoburn, J. (1991) *Permanent Family Placement.* BAAF.

Goldstein, J., Freud, A. and Solnit, A. J. (1973) *Beyond the Best Interests of the Child.* Free Press.

Goldstein, J., Freud, A. and Solnit, A. J. (1980) *Before the Best Interests of the Child.* Free Press.

Jewett, C. (1984) *Helping Children Cope with Separation and Loss.* Batsford.

Kossonen, M. (1996) Maintaining Sibling Relationships: Neglected Dimension in Child Care Practice. *British Journal of Social Work.* 26:6.

Lowe, N., Murch, M., Borkowski, M., Weaver, A., Beckford, V. and Thomas, C. (1999) *Supporting Adoption: Reframing the Approach.* BAAF.

Macaskill, C. (1985) *Against the Odds: Adopting Children with Disabilities.* BAAF.

Macaskill, C. (1991) *Adopting or Fostering A Sexually Abused Child.* Free Association Press.

McRoy, R. (1991) American Experience and Research on Openness. *Adoption and Fostering.* 15(4).

Mullender, A. (1999) *We are Family: Sibling Relationships in Placement and Beyond.* BAAF.

Quinton, D., Rushton, A., Dance, C. and Mayes, D. (1997) Contact Between Children Placed Away from Home and their Birth Parents: Research Issues and Evidence. *Clinical Child Psychology and Psychiatry.*

Quinton, D., Rushton, A., Dance, C. and Mayes, D. (1998) *Joining New Families; Adoption and Fostering in Middle Childhood.* Wiley.

Rowe, J. and Lambert, L. (1973) *Children who Wait.* Association of British Adoption Agencies.

Rushton, A., Dance, C., Quinton, D. and Mayes, D. (2001) *Siblings in Late Permanent Placement.* BAAF.

Ryburn, M. (1992) *Adoption in the 1990s: Identity and Openness.* Leamington Press.

Ryburn, M. (Ed.) (1994) Open Adoption: Research Therapy and Practice. Aldershot: Avebury.

Ryburn, M. (1998) In Whose Best Interests? Post Adoption Contact with the Birth Family. *Child and Family Law Quarterly.* 10:1.

Smith, G. (1995) Do Children have a Right to Leave their Pasts Behind them? in Argent, H. (Ed.) *See You Soon: Contact with Children Looked After by Local Authorities.* BAAF.

Social Services Inspectorate (1995) *Moving the Goalposts: A Study of Post Adoption Contact in the North of England.* London, Department of Health.

Triseliotis, J. (1973) *In Search of Origins.* Routledge and Kegan Paul.

Triseliotis, J. (1983) Identity and Security in Adoption and Long-term Fostering. *Adoption and Fostering.* 7:1, 22–31.

Triseliotis, J. (1985) Adoption and Contact. *Adoption and Fostering.* 9(4).

Wedge, P. and Mantle, G. (1991) *Sibling Groups and Social Work: A Study of Children Referred for Permanent Substitute Placement.* Aldershot, Avebury.

Agencies that Participated in the Research Study

Statutory Agencies

Camden Social Services
Enfield Social Services
Nottinghamshire Social Services

Voluntary Adoption Agencies

Adoption NCH (South East)
Barnardo's Jigsaw Project London
Barnardo's Derwen Project Cardiff
Coram Family Adoption Service London
Independent Adoption Service London
Parents For Children London
    Adoption UK also assisted in this project by identifying black families who were registered on their computerised database.

Guidance for Agencies

Criteria for Selection of Families

(a) All the children selected for study require to have been at least four years old at the time of placement. In the case of sibling groups at least one child should have been four at placement. The other siblings could be younger.

(b) The placement requires to have been made on a permanent basis in the first instance. This includes long term fostering as well as adoption. Do not include placements where the original plan was short term fostering or respite care and the family later decided to proceed to permanence.

(c) Exclude children with specific learning difficulties who have limited verbal ability. Include children who have suffered emotional trauma. Although it is recognised that many children in this category may have difficulties with learning, some degree of verbal ability is essential if children are going to be able to participate directly in the study.

(d) The child requires to have had at least one face-to-face contact with a member of the birth family since placement. Contact may be ongoing or it may have terminated.

(e) The term birth family should be interpreted more broadly than a birth parent and includes any member of the extended family e.g. sibling, grandparent, aunt or uncle.

Steps to Follow

(a) Working backwards from 1999 select all families who meet the above criteria (until the number of placements agreed with the researcher has been identified). Do not include any placements prior to 1990.

(b) Include placements that have disrupted as well as those that are ongoing.

A Guide to Good Practice on Face-to-Face Contact in Permanent Placements

This guide to good practice is based on the perceptions of adopters, foster carers, social workers, children and young people who participated in this research project.

- All parties who are involved in contact need to be fully consulted about contact plans. In any contact plan the needs of the child must be paramount but it is also important that the plan is practically manageable for everyone involved. Negative attitudes to the plan from any of the parties involved are likely to impinge unhelpfully on contact meetings and create torn loyalties within the child.
- It is essential that social workers invest time with children listening to their wishes about contact. One way of doing this is through the use of Life Story work. Children need to be able to grapple with why certain professional decisions about contact are made especially when these decisions do not concur exactly with their expressed wishes.
- Some adopters and foster carers may need help to understand how their own personal childhood experiences of trauma and loss can impinge unhelpfully on a child's contact plan. This issue should be explored by social workers with all fostering and adoption applicants.
- When children have suffered abuse within their birth family, it is important to undertake a risk analysis of the current or potential links that exist between the birth relatives who are planning to retain contact and the wider abusive network. An appropriate degree of confidentiality for the child must be included in the plan. It is important to consider the long term as well as the immediate risks associated with confidentiality.
- Contact plans must be underpinned by a financial budget and resource implications need to be addressed and agreed from the outset.

- A clearly defined contact plan needs to be negotiated between social workers and all the parties at the beginning of the placement rather than leaving the plan to evolve in an *ad hoc* manner between the adults. Having clear boundaries surrounding a contact plan is one way of protecting a child's best interests.
- Following negotiation between a social worker and all the parties, a written contact agreement needs to be established. It should be specific and cover the issues that are detailed in Chapter 3 (see page 41, content of written contact agreements). It is helpful to have this written agreement prepared prior to embarking on initial contact meetings although the plan is likely to require adaptation as it moves from theory to practice and as the needs of different parties change and develop.
- An introductory meeting between the adults who are to be involved in contact is crucial prior to the first contact meeting involving the child. A positive and sensitive relationship between the adults is crucial to the ongoing success of contact and therefore this meeting is foundational to what happens in future contact meetings. Attempting to create shortcuts by omitting this stage of the process is likely to have a detrimental effect on ongoing contact plans.
- Careful consideration should be given to the timing of the first contact meeting following placement. When birth relatives approve of the placement it can be reassuring for the child to have the first contact meeting just a few weeks after placement. When the birth relatives do not approve of the placement it is essential to delay the first contact meeting for several months to enable the child to form a secure bond with their new family without the emotional upheaval of torn loyalties.
- Preparing the child for contact is vital. It is imperative that all parties are clear about the names that will be used during contact meetings. The terms 'mum' and 'dad' are likely to arouse particularly strong emotional responses from birth relatives. In order to reduce tension for the child it is crucial that all parties accept beforehand the names that will be used. Some children may benefit from role playing the contact meeting prior to embarking on it. Others who cannot tolerate any degree of disturbance to their regular routine may find it helpful to have every minute detail about what is going to happen from the beginning to the end of a contact meeting written down in simple language for them.
- It is essential that at least one adopter or permanent foster carer attend contact meetings during the early phases of any new also

placement. This will provide the child with a sense of security and convey a clear message to the child about who is the primary parent figure. It is also a way of demonstrating an important message to the child about continuity between their past and present. This is essential for children whose lives have frequently been marked by disintegration and fragmentation.

- Care needs to be taken when considering what type of contact venue to use. It is particularly easy to rush into using the adopter's home because it is a convenient and relaxed setting. However this venue may not provide adequate long-term safeguards for the child in relation to confidentiality. Using the birth relative's geographical location for contact meetings may result in some children and teenagers being preoccupied with fears about a surprise encounter with other birth relatives who have perpetrated abuse in the past.

- Suitable neutral venues for contact meetings are a scarce resource. There is a need for such venues to be established.

- It is important that the frequency of contact is established at a level that is manageable for all parties. The age, developmental level and emotional resilience of the child need to be taken into account and also the attitudes of the adults. When face-to-face contact is established in adoption placements at a level beyond four times annually it is liable to be unsustainable. It is also important to remember that contact meetings between children and their birth parents that are set at a level of once annually create a different type of pressure for children because contact becomes a major event that is outside the child's norm. The protracted period between meetings provides the child with scope to fantasise about their birth family.

- Positive relationships between foster carers or adopters and birth relatives help children to manage the dilemma of having 'two families'. Evidence of positive partnerships between the adults in both families during contact meetings through the exchange of kind words and simple generous deeds are deeply meaningful to children and provide tangible and visible proof to them that a positive relationship does exist.

- Some birth relatives will need a lot of preparation and support in order to ensure that they convey an accepting rather than a rejecting attitude towards the child. Rejecting attitudes from birth parents can result in children suffering further emotional harm.

- Children who have suffered trauma in their birth family are likely to experience a range of positive and negative conflicting emotions during and after contact meetings. Children need help to express these very confusing emotions and to make sense of such turbulent feelings that can be overwhelming.

- Teenagers who are well established in their new placements are likely to find it difficult to have their adopters present with them at contact meetings with their birth parents. Managing the reality of relating to 'two parents' simultaneously is likely to evoke high levels of turbulence for teenagers. Could a suitable neutral person be identified to accompany them during such an emotive encounter? A pilot scheme could be established whereby suitable volunteers could be trained to take on this role.

- It is a mistake to automatically terminate arrangements for formal supervision of contact as significant milestones are reached in a child's life like the granting of an Adoption Order or a foster child attaining the age of 18 years. The issue of supervision has resource implications. The question of who should provide supervision needs to be re-evaluated by professionals. (see Chapter 8 page 134, Summary of Key Points: Supervision)

- A contact plan should never be static. Instead it should have a creative and dynamic quality inherent in it. There is a need to introduce a review system for contact plans in adoption which could be accessed by any of the parties when contact plans need to be adapted to meet changing circumstances.

- At every phase in the contact plan the availability of an intermediary is important. This person can provide brokerage between the different parties and help to relieve tensions between people who have a high level of emotional investment in what is happening. The availability of an intermediary will play a significant part in ensuring that contact plans are sustained in the long term.

- A continuing support service is essential for all parties. It must extend beyond adoption. The availability of a named post holder within social services with responsibility for post adoption issues will facilitate access to support on contact issues beyond adoption. A proportion of children with complex histories are likely to require specialist psychotherapeutic services and such specialist provision needs to be pre planned. Ways of opening up opportunities for adopted and foster children to interact with others who have had personal experience of adoption or fostering and contact with their birth relatives should be considered.

Acknowledgements

This publication would not have been possible without the help of several people: Karen Irving, Chief Executive, and the Executive Committee of *Parents for Children* who agreed to fund a considerable proportion of this research study: the social work staff of other statutory and voluntary adoption agencies who also participated and gave generously of their time to identify a research sample: adoptive parents, foster carers, children and young people who agreed to be interviewed and were prepared to share their personal views and feelings on this sensitive subject. Staff at Adoption UK also assisted by attempting to identify additional black families who were registered on their database.

A key person who was involved in this project from the outset was Shelagh Beckett. Shelagh was initially nominated by *Parents For Children* to supervise the research. She continued to give voluntarily of her time and commitment to the work when financial sponsorship underpinning the project was terminated. Shelagh's clarity of thought and thorough supervision has been invaluable.

Special thanks is also extended to Tamara Hallam and Lucy Cork who prepared Ben's Story, the research tool that was used for interviewing children and young people. Tamara and Lucy prepared this research tool when they were undertaking a practice placement at *Parents for Children* as part of their DipSW training course. Amira Alam from Barnardos Derwen Project Cardiff also made a unique contribution by sharing her personal perspective about racial issues. I am also grateful to Carolyn Gumley for her efficient preparation of the charts used in the manuscript.

Ann Wheal, working on behalf of Russell House Publishing has also played a significant role in ensuring that this publication became a reality. I am grateful to Ann for reading and commenting on the draft manuscript and to Geoffrey Mann and Martin Jones at Russell House Publishing for their specialist advice and consultation as the manuscript progressed through various stages towards publication.

On a personal level, I would like to thank my husband Calum for his endless patience, encouragement and practical support during the entire period when I worked on the publication. I am also very grateful to my special friends David and Muriel Lacey for helping me to reach a level of computer literacy that was essential for the preparation of this research material for publication.

Confidentiality
All the names of children and adults who participated in this study have been changed for the purposes of confidentiality.